A Gospel to Proclaim

A Gospel to Proclaim

Nigel McCulloch

Foreword by George Carey

Darton, Longman and Todd
London

First published in 1992 by
Darton, Longman and Todd Ltd
89 Lillie Road, London SW6 1UD

ISBN 0–232–52007–0

A catalogue record for this book is available
from the British Library

Cover design by Leigh Hurlock

Phototypeset by Intype, London
Printed and bound in Great Britain
at the University Press, Cambridge

*During this Decade of Evangelism
the Churches are challenged to work together
to make Christ known
to the people of his world:*

Praying *for the renewing love and power of the Holy Spirit*
Equipping *all Christians to live and share the Gospel*
Exploring *God's activity in different situations and cultures*
Changing *wherever necessary the Church's worship,
ministry and structures*
Confronting *injustice and responding to human need*
Proclaiming *the Gospel by word and deed*

Based on an official statement from
the Decade of Evangelism Steering Group

Contents

Foreword

The final decade of a millennium will inevitably be the focus of conflicting emotions. As we approach the year 2000, there is a sense that we are entering a new era. It is this rather unfocused feeling which the so called New Age movement has tapped.

The Christian Churches are also conscious that the year 2000 has significance for them. What shape will they be in when the third millennium of the Christian era dawns? There may be more Christians in the world in the 1990s than ever before, but there has been also an undeniable loss of confidence in some parts of the Christian family, especially in the West.

The Decade of Evangelism is the Church's own reply to its self questioning. It is the means of drawing attention to one of the Church's primary tasks at what is felt to be a crucial time for the future of Christianity. This book describes how the Decade came to be adopted by the Anglican Communion, and gives an excellent account of the ways in which the Church of England in particular is responding.

I had the privilege of working with Nigel McCulloch in the diocese of Bath and Wells. His enthusiasm and energy are infectious, and they come across in the pages of this book. But he is the first to recognise that enthusiasm and energy are not enough for evangelism to be effective. It must have its roots in prayer and worship, and in the recognition that this is God's mission, not ours. Even St Paul felt that we were 'no better than pots of earthenware to contain this treasure' (2 Corinthians 4:7), and the treasure of which he spoke was the revelation of the glory of God in the face of Jesus Christ. That remains our treasure today, and it is not a treasure to keep to ourselves, but to proclaim as the year 2000 approaches.

+ GEORGE CANTUAR

Introduction

The purpose of this book is to open some windows, in the hope that others will be able to see out more clearly. I view the Decade of Evangelism with a mixture of genuine commitment to proclaiming the Gospel and a healthy questioning about how it is to be done.

In trying to explain why we are in a Decade of Evangelism, what it means, and how it is progressing, I have become increasingly aware that there is nothing so complicated as trying to pass on the simple message of God's love!

My personal commitment to, and enthusiasm for, evangelism is rooted in my experience over twelve years as a parish priest – first as curate in a northern industrial parish, and then as incumbent of St Thomas's, Salisbury. As a chaplain in a university I valued the rigorous intellectual testing which invariably met the proclaiming of the Gospel.

As diocesan missioner and later bishop in two largely rural dioceses, I came to sympathise with clergy and congregations who sometimes felt exhausted and dispirited by the ideas, demands and expectations which seemed to come in an endless stream 'from above'. During my enthronement service at Wakefield I was surprised to be interrupted by spontaneous applause. It came after these words: 'There is too much busyness in our Church at present: too much rushing around, too many committees, too much paper circulated. It all points to the disease of activism which is infecting us all.'

That is why I have stressed in this book that, in my view, the Decade of Evangelism ought not to be about doing a lot more things. I want to resist that. What is needed is a major change of attitude and emphasis in the life of the Church and the lives of its members. We need to be freed from being a Church which is forever absorbed in churchy things: then we may come nearer to being a Church which is Christlike.

* * *

I am grateful for the prayers and support of the staff of the Board of Mission and the Steering Group – especially Marion Mort, without whose advice, encouragement and energy I would never have written this book. My chaplain, Roy Clements, has made many valuable suggestions which have been enormously helpful. Celia, my wife, has given me unfailing love, support and patience as I have tried to combine the first months of ministry in a new diocese with an attempt to be an author.

Last, but by no means least, I want to pay tribute to the Archbishop of Canterbury, Dr George Carey, for the strong and visionary leadership he is giving to the Church of England in this Decade of Evangelism. The Church of England, the nation, and the Anglican Communion are greatly blessed in having a courageous leader, who is warm and approachable, and has a deep spiritual commitment to proclaiming the Gospel.

NIGEL MCCULLOCH
Bishop's Lodge, Wakefield
St Thomas's Day, 1992

1

The Challenge

The Right Moment

Controversy there may be, but one thing is certain: nothing in recent years has so captured the imagination of the Church of England as the ecumenical Decade of Evangelism. We are a Church on the move.

After years of pessimism and decline, Anglicans are becoming more confident about their faith and its relevance in helping them face up to the disillusion and materialism of so much of our society. There is a fresh and exciting commitment to being the missionary Church we are always supposed to have been since the Day of Pentecost.

The challenge to a decade of evangelism in these last ten years of the century came from the bishops of the Anglican Communion in 1988, when they met for their ten-yearly Lambeth Conference. But it takes more than a Lambeth Call to affect the people in the pew. Why then has this particular call had such an impact in England?

Part of the answer lies in a comment Stephen Mumba, the Bishop of Lusaka in Zambia, made even before the Conference had assembled. Like many of the bishops from abroad, he took the opportunity to call on parishes he had visited on an earlier trip here. What he found surprised him. In a sermon early that July he put it like this: 'Something is happening to the Church of England. It is changing. I see signs of new life.'

Other visiting bishops said the same thing. The Church of England they had seen in sad decline and some disarray in the 1960s and 1970s seemed to be showing signs of recovering its nerve. But there was still room for improvement. Dinis Sengulane, the Bishop of Lebombo in Mozambique, asked: 'Why do some of your congregations in England look so miserable? I have a message for them from Africa. Cheer up!'

Renewal

Overall however, by 1988 the Church of England was feeling more cheerful than it had done for some years. Why? Part of the reason was the new and more relaxed worship encouraged by the 1980 Alternative Service Book – not least the increasingly popular 'family serves' with their free and creative style. A further, and often significant, cause of optimism was the growing influence during the 1980s of the charismatic renewal movement especially, but by no means only, in the evangelical wing of the Church. In the eight years prior to 1988, the style and content of worship in many parish churches had altered far more than most regular worshippers realised.

Faith in the City

Another enlivening influence on the Church of England in the 1980s was the publication in 1986 of the *Faith in the City* report. Not only did this bring to the fore the prophetic voice of the Church within the nation, but through the Church Urban Fund it galvanised into action almost every parish church in the land. The Fund, which had been recommended in the report, was launched in early 1988 as a practical expression of faith in action – the Church living out the Gospel. The focus was on the poorest, the forgotten and the ignored – especially in those places designated as Urban Priority Areas. As with most fund-raising projects, when there is a clear aim in view people respond, and the Church Urban Fund was no exception. It captured the imagination of church members and highlighted the responsibility of all Christians for the poor and deprived within our communities.

In their different ways these two features of the Church of England's life in the 1980s brought vision, energy and a sense of purpose to its members. The new and lively worship and the new commitment to the disadvantaged showed the Church both affirming its part in drawing people to personal salvation and its involvement in social action. It was to be a crucial element in the foundation on which the Decade of Evangelism, at any rate, for the Church of England, was to be built.

The Ground Prepared

By 1988 there was, as the Bishop of Lusaka rightly observed, a new spirit in the air, and it was not confined to the Church of England, nor even to Anglicanism. During the same period the Roman Catholic Church had been preparing to mark the turn of the millennium. In 1987 Pope John Paul II announced that the last ten years of the century would be a Decade of Evangelisation. In Roman Catholicism, as in Protestantism, those involved in charismatic renewal were making plans to encourage and enable Christians of all denominations to pass on their faith to others.

It was against this background that the bishops of the Anglican Communion met for the Lambeth Conference of 1988. There was no plan for a Decade of Evangelism as such on the agenda, but a good deal of thinking about mission had gone on before it. Three years earlier, a significant report entitled *Giving Mission its Proper Place* had been produced by the Church of England's Board of Mission and Unity, and this proved to be influential in the thinking for the Ministry and Mission section of the Conference. As Bishop Michael Nazir-Ali, one of the theological consultants to the Lambeth Conference, observed, even before the bishops met, the preparatory papers and consultations were moving to a position which would challenge the conference on the subject of evangelism.

Enthusiasm Kindled

Bishop Michael Nazir-Ali's account of how the Decade Resolutions came about counters the popular view that it was the African bishops who first suggested it. It has been said that the African bishops got tired of what they regarded as an American-European dominated agenda, and passionately urged the whole Communion to share their own enthusiasm for evangelism – pointing out that the fastest-growing Anglican congregations are in Africa. The bishop claims that it was in fact the Americans who had the thoughts of the Decade of Evangelism uppermost in their minds. They came to Lambeth almost directly from their General Convention, which had just approved a resolution on the Decade brought to it from its own Commission on Evangelism. In an article in the *Church Times*, Bishop Nazir-Ali wrote:

> If the Americans had come prepared, the Africans and others were not slow to take up the challenge. A conference plenary which heard about evangelisation in Africa, Asia and Europe had the result of kindling further enthusiasm. The concern quickly found support among a wide cross-section of the participants. It was never a case of one group foisting its enthusiasms on others. This is perhaps the reason why the resolution has found such wide support in the churches of the Anglican Communion. A subject previously almost taboo in some Anglican circles in increasingly discussed and acted on at every level of church life.

The Resolutions

Like most conferences, Lambeth 1988 produced its resolutions – a large number of them. Probably none will turn out to have had such influence as numbers 43 and 44. Resolution 43, entitled 'Decade of Evangelism' states:

This Conference, recognising that evangelism is the primary task given to the Church, asks each Province and diocese of the Anglican Communion, in co-operation with other Christians, to make the closing years of this millennium a 'Decade of Evangelism', with a renewed and united emphasis on making Christ known to the people of his world.

(It is unfortunate that evangelism is here called 'the' primary task of the Church. Evangelism is, without doubt, 'a' primary task of the church; but 'the' primary task, for which it exists, is to worship God. It is from that that all else flows.)

Resolution 44 is headed 'Evangelism in the Anglican Communion'. It reads:

This conference:

1. Calls for a shift to a dynamic missionary emphasis going beyond care and nurture to proclamation and service; and therefore,

2. Accepts the challenge this presents to diocesan and local church structures and patterns of worship and ministry, and looks to God for a fresh movement of the Spirit in prayer, outgoing love and evangelism in obedience to our Lord's command.

The bishops were in no doubt about the size of the task they were calling the Anglican churches to undertake. In the Conference Report on Mission and Ministry the wording is of the need for a 'massive' shift to a mission outlook. It is clear that what is required is not a series of special mission activities in the local churches, but something much more fundamental. The Decade of Evangelism is about changing the whole outlook and attitude of the Church. The bishop is to be 'more than ever a leader in mission'; and if the Decade is to have a lasting impact then it will be necessary for 'the structure of dioceses, local churches, theological training, etc. [to] be so reshaped that they become instruments that generate missionary movement as well as pastoral care'.

Every Christian an Agent of Mission

The key resolution for implementing these hopes is number 42: 'This Conference recommends that Provinces and dioceses encourage, train, equip and send out lay people for evangelism and ministry.' That is the heart of the matter – what the documents call nothing less than a 'revolution in the attitude to the role of laity . . . which would enable us to see every Christian as an agent of mission'. If the laity are not seen as at the forefront of mission then the point of the Decade has been missed.

The Bishops' Reactions

Not all the bishops at Lambeth greeted the commitment to a Decade of Evangelism with immediate delight! Some were frankly gloomy and felt the whole thing was a mistake, although there was a feeling that one could hardly vote against evangelism.

One of the Australian bishops said he had not been set on fire at all by the idea. However, on his way home later he took a taxi, and the driver began talking to him. They were about the same age and they chatted about their grandchildren. The taxi driver then asked the bishop, who was not wearing any kind of clerical dress, whether he had a faith and went on to share in a very open but sensitive way his own faith and hopes for his grandchildren. The bishop reflected on the fact that here was a lay Christian, not in a privileged position, not trained in any special way, and certainly not a clergyman, who was doing what every Christian ought to do – passing on the good news of Jesus. The question the bishop was left with was: 'Why do I myself shrink from it?'

Church of England Committed

Whilst some of the English bishops were uneasy about the Decade Resolutions, most welcomed them. Later, the House of Bishops of the Church of England, whilst sounding some notes of caution, endorsed the call to evangelism, and the matter was referred to the General Synod. The record of debates that had taken place there on evangelism was not encouraging, and there were voices in Church House raising grave doubts about the wisdom of committing the Church of England to a Decade of Evangelism. However, in the event there was firm support from all sides of churchmanship and by 1989 the Church was both episcopally and synodically committed to take up the challenge. The green light was on.

The ball then landed in the court of the General Synod's Board of Mission and Unity, which had neither the money nor the staff to take on any extra work, so a Steering Group for the Decade was formed. Its membership included people from the varying shades of Anglican churchmanship and key representatives of the other main denominations. The task before the group was twofold – to encourage all the denominations to co-operate in the Decade and to advise on an appropriate launch.

From the start there was a high level of expectation and wisely tempered enthusiasm within the Steering Group. It quickly developed contacts in the field through the network of Diocesan Missioners and their equivalents and soon became the only national group capable of drawing together the wide range of thinking and planning for the imminent demise, the British Council of Churches asked the Steering Group to take over its own brief in relation to the launch of the Decade.

The Crescendo Policy

The Steering Group was worried that triumphalist and fundamentalist views might feature too prominently in the plans for the launch. There was also a growing concern that the media would give a big build-up to any official national launch – leading people to expect immediate results – only to knock it all down as a failure a year later. There emerged what has come to be known as 'the crescendo policy' – a relatively quiet start with a progressive build up each year through the decade and into the turn of the millennium.

The very fact that the Lambeth Conference, and other denominations, had felt it necessary to call for the Decade was, of course, a mark of the failure of the Church to be the missionary Church it was meant to be since the Day of Pentecost. That in itself was a very good reason why triumphalist tones were not appropriate for launching the Decade.

Over 100,000 Members of the Laity

Another powerful factor also influenced the Steering Group's decision to advise the churches against a major national launch. The emphasis in the Lambeth documents and resolutions had been on the laity and the local church, and many more lay people could be involved in launch services at diocesan and local levels. On dates near the official launch day – 6 January, the Feast of the Epiphany – over 100,000 people attended special ecumenical and diocesan launch services: almost every Christian congregation in the land was represented at these. In addition, tens of thousands were at similar acts of worship in their parish churches. The determination to avoid the spectacular, televisual national event, but to concentrate on the less news-catching but more deeply rooted local launches, has been a major factor in ensuring that, two years into the decade, evangelism is still firmly at the top of the agenda in very many local churches, and increasingly so.

Churches Together in England

We are not alone in this. Not only are we joining in a common undertaking with Anglicans across the world in what Colin Craston, Chairman of the Anglican Consultative Council, describes as 'the most significant movement for the whole Anglican Communion in modern times', but we are also joining other denominations. In 1991, the four presidents of the newly formed Churches Together in England (representing the Church of England, the Roman Catholic Church, the Free Church Federal Council and the Wesleyan Holiness Church) issued 'A Call to Pray for a Decade' to coincide with the local launch services on the first Sunday of the decade. They wrote:

> Every Christian has the duty and the joy of passing on to others the Good News of Jesus Christ. We are to be 'ambassadors for Christ' – sharing in his work, reflecting his likeness, and inviting others to join in the same pilgrimage. During the next ten years we are being asked to commit ourselves in love and service to others. As Christ binds up the brokenhearted and sets captives free, we are called to bring the message of his love to all, whether poor or powerful.
>
> The first Sunday of the year is the day on which many Christians renew their dedication to God's work. The first Sunday of this Decade also falls on the feast of the Epiphany which reminds us that Christ is for all the nations. His good news speaks to each of us individually but it also speaks to whole communities. Wherever it is received, it brings hope to situations of division and despair, and affirms all that is just and pure. We are called to dedicate ourselves anew to spread this word, and to prepare the way for the coming of his Kingdom of justice on earth.
>
> But the Church itself must listen to Christ. We, too, need to hear the Gospel afresh, be touched by its challenge and its power and continually transformed by its message.

Churches Together in England has begun a new way for

Christians to work together in our country. It is right that our first common undertaking should be to evangelise. We wish to join with you in making the next ten years a time in which our priority is to live, to proclaim and to teach the gospel. Let us also pray that we may all grow to a deeper unity formed by the Spirit, so that the world may believe in Christ, and through him come to worship to the Father.

No Going Back

For the Church of England, there can be no going back on this Decade of Evangelism. We are deeply and utterly committed to it, not just through the House of Bishops and General Synod, but because we have made the undertaking in company with our fellow Anglicans in our Communion and with our fellow Christians in other denominations.

A decade of evangelism is a costly undertaking. It demands a deeper life of prayer on the part of Christians, as well as the ability to articulate simply the articles of the Christian faith. It requires us to be prepared to change the forms and shape of our religious observance, to make them more accessible to those who are unfamiliar with them. It means challenging the secular goals of personal advancement and self-interest with the Gospel ideals of self-sacrifice and a mutually caring community. It expects us to approach scientific issues and social concerns, not with a blind fundamentalism that denies reality, but with a steadfast faith in God's unconditional love and the values embodied in the earthly ministry of Jesus. It called us to build up trust and form relationships with those who do not share our culture or our faith, and to do so in ways which do not threaten or demean what they hold dear, yet do not compromise our Christian allegiance. We must witness to our faith by our very manner.

If we believe that the man who stumbled over the cobble-stones of old Jerusalem on the way to a painful and degrading death on Calvary was and is the Son of God – who rose from the dead and invites us in our generation to share in his work of reconciling all created things to their creator – then we have no option but to accept the invitation to become his ambassadors and equip ourselves for the task. Already, up and down the country, that work has begun; there is indeed a new spirit in the air. Christians really are finding fresh ways of proclaiming the story of God's love, and each week more churches of almost every denomination are taking up the challenge 'to work together to make Christ known to the people of his world'.

2

Praying

More Than an Extra Item on the Agenda

Two churches I know were asked by the bishop to prepare for the Decade of Evangelism, and he asked them to let him know how they planned to respond to the challenge of making Christ known in their parishes. The approach of each church was very different. One added it on to the agenda of the next Parochial Church Council meeting. It was discussed at the end of the evening after a long and difficult debate about the quota payment. Not surprisingly, the vicar told the bishop he could detect no enthusiasm for the Decade among his people. The other church decided that before any discussion took place there should be a prayer vigil for members of the congregation to seek the Lord's guidance about the way ahead. That vicar reported a deep and moving readiness on the part of his people to be open to whatever the Spirit might be saying to them in this decade.

If the vision of making Christ known to the people of his world is to become a reality, it will not be achieved by simply adding the Decade on as an extra item on the agenda – nor even just by attending training programmes and learning evangelistic techniques. It will happen when the hearts and minds of the laity and clergy, our synods and councils, are open to the renewing love and power of the Holy Spirit.

Prayer the Priority

Remember how the first decade of evangelism began on the
Day of Pentecost. The story in Acts 2 is dramatic and well
known. The early believers were sitting together when suddenly
the house they were in was filled with a noise which sounded
like a strong wind. It seemed as if tongues of fire touched
everyone there, and they were all filled with the Holy Spirit
and began to talk in other languages.

Less familiar is a crucial verse which comes in the previous
chapter. In Acts 1:14 we are told: 'They [the apostles] joined
in continuous prayer, together with the women and with Mary
the mother of Jesus and with his brothers'. There can be no
doubting that the backcloth to the first decade of evangelism
was an intensity of prayer.

The story of the Day of Pentecost records that such was the
effect of the coming of the Holy Spirit on the apostles that
some of the onlookers made fun of them for being drunk. Thus
was Peter prompted to give the first recorded sermon in the
history of the Christian Church, explaining that they were not
drunk but filled with the Holy Spirit.

> God has raised this very Jesus from death, and we are all
> witnesses to this fact. He has been raised to the right-hand
> side of God, his Father, and has received from him the Holy
> Spirit, as he had promised. What you now see and hear is
> his gift that he has poured out on us.
>
> (Acts 2:32–3)

Clear Message and Prayerful Nurture

Peter's sermon is a classic example of evangelistic preaching.
It led those who were listening to make a response. No sooner
has he ended with the climax, 'know for sure that this Jesus,
whom you crucified, is the one that God has made Lord and
Messiah', than they became worried and asked, 'What shall we

do?' Peter's answer was clear and it had provided the pattern for much of subsequent evangelism: 'Each one of you must turn away from his sins and be baptised in the name of Jesus Christ, so that your sins will be forgiven; and you will receive God's gift, the Holy Spirit' (Acts 2:38).

The result was that many believed what Peter was saying. On the first Day of Pentecost there were about 3,000 new Christians. Note how they were integrated. It was a fourfold programme:

1. they learned from the apostles about Jesus
2. they took part in the fellowship
3. they shared in the meals
4. they prayed together.

That, together with the evangelistic preaching of the apostles, led to further dramatic results. Every day the Lord added to their group those who were being saved.

It is abundantly clear that before the first decade of evangelism began the apostles and those with them were in a state of constant prayer – waiting for guidance. It is equally clear that, from the moment they were engaged in their evangelistic task, they and their numerous new companions based everything they did on prayerful fellowship. Thus did the Holy Spirit enable the Church to grow.

Evidence of Increased Prayer

The current Decade of Evangelism will quickly collapse unless it continues in prayer. There is no doubt that the atmosphere at the various launch services around the country was often deeply prayerful. Many dioceses produced special prayer cards and bookmarks. Others had a special time set aside for prayer and one diocese now has an annual prayer vigil for the decade each Petertide. Others have produced prayer material for use in parishes, using tapes.

In the Chichester Diocese 11,000 people have used the ecu-

PRAYING 15

menical course, 'Praying Together for the New Evangelisation'.
The Winchester Diocese has distributed 35,000 copies of its
leaflet 'Waiting on God with the Jesus Prayer', which is also
available on tape for the blind. Prayer schools across the
country have often been oversubscribed: around 700 members
of the laity have attended them in Blackburn alone. The Here-
ford Diocese has produced a simple office for individuals to
use in a parish at an agreed time each day: well over 4,000
have been distributed. Prayer meetings and prayer and praise
sessions were key elements in the preparations for the major
ecumenical evangelistic celebration in Leeds. Prayer Triplets,
where people meet in groups of three to pray, are increasingly
used in connection with parish evangelism such as 'Good News
Down the Street'.

Many Anglican Church leaders would agree with the sum-
ming up of one diocese: 'Spiritual renewal must take place
prior to, or simultaneously with, evangelism, and there are very
hopeful signs that such renewal is taking place.'

Listening and Giving

The Steering Group was convinced from the earliest days of
the preparations that prayer lay at the heart of evangelism. It
was no accident that the first official publication it produced
for the decade was a collection of prayers entitled *Prayers for
a Decade*. Drawn from a rich variety of sources, modern as
well as traditional, there are prayers for use by individuals or
small groups, with a different theme for each day of the week.
The booklet contains special readings and prayers for Holy
Communion, an outline for a Family Service, and the Method-
ist Covenant prayer used in that denomination's powerful
annual commitment to God's service. The compilation is the
work of Brother Bernard, whose Franciscan insights have been
very influential in the Church of England's response to the
Decade – not least in rooting it in an authentically Anglican
spirituality. Two of his own prayers have been widely used:

> Set us free, O God,
> to cross barriers for you,
> as you crossed barriers for us
> in Jesus Christ our Lord. Amen.

> Spirit of God,
> make us open to others in listening,
> generous to others in giving,
> and sensitive to others in praying;
> through Jesus Christ our Lord. Amen.

The Disease of Activism

Valuable as all these spiritual resources are proving to be, a few extra prayers and special themes for services are not enough. One of the hopes I cherish for this decade is that the Church of England will become a more visibly prayerful Church. There is far too much busyness at present – too much rushing around, too many committees; the disease of activism is infecting us all. We all need a still centre to our lives and to calm down so that we can wait on what the Spirit is saying to us. Before it is anything else, the Decade of Evangelism is a call to prayer. Unfortunately, far too many people have interpreted the decade as being primarily about doing more things. It cannot be said too often that it is about something far more fundamental – nothing less than the transformation of attitudes and outlooks. A local church which sees the Decade of Evangelism as yet one more burden imposed on already overworked shoulders is missing the point. The prayerful words of John Greenleaf Whittier put it well:

> Drop Thy still dews of quietness
> Till all our strivings cease
> Take from our souls the strain and stress
> And let our ordered lives confess
> The beauty of thy peace.

Becoming Like Christ

The primary task of the Church is to worship God. Now, perhaps more than ever before, the Church needs to be – and be seen to be – a Church at prayer. Then, instead of being thought to be constantly absorbed in churchy things, we may become a Church which is increasingly seen to be Christ-like. That vision was expressed beautifully by the sixteenth-century Spanish Carmelite nun and mystic, St Teresa of Avila:

Christ has no body now on earth but yours
No hands but yours
No feet but yours
Yours are the eyes through which Christ's compassion
is to look out on the world
Yours are the feet with which he is to go about doing good
And yours are the hands with which he is to bless now.

Therein lies a key point about evangelism and what it means to become the forefront missionaries of the Church. We are called not just follow Jesus, but to become daily more like him, so that, in this generation and in this Decade of Evangelism, we can be his eyes and feet and hands.

Seeing Christ in Others

Christian spirituality has much to teach us about our approach to other people. Speaking from within the Benedictine tradition, Cardinal Hume has said: 'Each person is made in the image of God. That means that every time I meet someone I learn a little more about God.' St Benedict's two very simple questions asked after people had visited his community need to be remembered by everyone who seeks to pass on the good news of Jesus Christ to others. 'Did we see Christ in them?' and 'Did they see Christ in us?'

John Wesley's Spirituality

Few evangelists have had the lasting effect on people's lives
that John Wesley's ministry achieved during the fifty years
leading up to his death in 1791. His stated aim was 'to promote
as far as I am able vital practical religion and by the grace of
God to beget, preserve and increase the life of God in the souls
of men'. It is not always realised that his evangelistic ministry
was deeply rooted in his reading not only of the scriptures but
of some of the great spiritual writers. He counted Thomas à
Kempis, the fourteenth-century author of the *Imitation of
Christ* among his favourites. William Law's *A Serious Call to
a Devout and Holy Life*, written in 1728, also deeply influenced
him. Indeed, apart from John Bunyan's *Pilgrim's Progress*,
William Law's *Serious Call* has probably been more influential
than any other post-Reformation spiritual book. Wesley also
valued highly the two key devotional works of the seventeenth-
century bishop Jeremy Taylor, *The Rule and Exercise of Holy
Living* and *The Rule and Exercise of Holy Dying*. These are
classic expressions of Anglican spirituality, with their emphasis
on ordered living and moderation in all things.

The importance of all this, from the point of view of this
current Decade of Evangelism, is to see that John Wesley's
evangelistic impact was not the result of shallow enthusiasm.
There is a danger – indeed it is already evident – that some
modern evangelism is so lacking in spiritual roots that it lacks
both integrity and authenticity. Wesley's ministry was deeply
rooted in all that he had learned from his favourite spiritual
writers. It was in his prayer room at home that he communed
with God and prayed for the renewing love and power of the
Holy Spirit. It was from that firm and secure foundation that
he went out to make Christ known to the people of his world
and passed on the good news that no-one is ever beyond the
reach of the loving and saving power of Jesus.

Love – Not Aggression

There is always a danger that, in passing on the good news of
Jesus, Christians may be insensitive and even aggressive. It is
worth noting that, among the anniversaries commemorated in
the year in which the current Decade of Evangelism was
launched, was that of the Spanish saint, St John of the Cross,
who died 400 years ago in 1591. One of Christianity's greatest
mystical theologians and poets, his experience of despair and
seeming rejection by God led him to write about what he called
'the dark night of the soul'. His lyrical poetry, which has come
to have an increasingly commanding influence on Christian
spirituality, is summed up in the title of another of his major
works: *The Living Flame of Love*. St John of the Cross is
sometimes described as the poet of Christian love, and that his
anniversary should coincide with the launch of a Decade of
Evangelism is entirely fitting. We need to be reminded that
love is the very essence of what we are about.

That theme, so important to evangelism, is evident in Anglican spirituality too. Few poems are more profound and beauti-
ful expressions of that than the seventeenth-century poet
George Herbert's *Love*. Simone Weil, the twentieth-century
mystic, said that once, when reading it, 'Christ himself came
down and took possession of me'. The poet expresses the sense
of inadequacy felt by those called by Jesus. Could he really
accept the call? Was he good enough? This conflict is resolved
in a dialogue between Love – that is Jesus – and the poet:

> Love bade me welcome; yet my soul drew back,
> Guilty of dust and sin.
> But quick-eyed Love, observing me grow slack
> From my first entrance in,
> Drew nearer to me, sweetly questioning,
> If I lacked anything.
>
> 'A guest', I answered, 'worthy to be here.'
> Love said, 'You shall be he.'
> 'I, the unkind, ungrateful? Ah, my dear,

I cannot look on thee.'
Love took my hand, and smiling, did reply,
'Who made the eyes but I?'

'Truth, Lord, but I have marred them; let my shame
Go where it doth deserve.'
'And know you not', says Love, 'who bore the blame?'
'My dear, then I will serve.'
'You must sit down', says Love, 'and taste my meat.'
So I did sit and eat.

A Rich Spiritual Resource

The Christian Church has a rich resource of spirituality to offer
those who are searching to find the answer to their deep and
often unarticulated questions about the meaning and purpose
of life. More members of the laity are associating themselves
with religious communities and their spirituality by becoming,
for example, members of the Third Order of the Franciscans
or of the Oblates of the Order of St Benedict. Those who do
this are required to live their lives according to a modified
Rule of Life that embraces worship and lifestyle. The religious
communities are making a significant and increasing contribution to the Decade by strengthening its spiritual under-
girding.

There is no doubt that imaginations have been caught and
lives helped by a wide range of spiritual initiatives in recent
years – and all these are being given a higher profile now that
we are in a Decade of Evangelism. Most Church of England
dioceses offer a variety of approaches. There are the increasingly popular and often packed Cathedral Prayer and Praise
services organised by the charismatic Anglican Renewal Ministries. Some parishes have been deeply influenced by John
Wimber. Increasing numbers of both laity and clergy have
found the Cursillo movement has brought new life into their
own spirituality. Ignatian Retreats, following in varying degrees

the Spiritual Exercises of St Ignatius Loyola, draw growing numbers from all denominations.

Centres of Spiritual Renewal

The increase in the number of people going on retreats and quiet days may turn out to be one of the most significant features of renewed church life in this Decade. Never have the Retreat Houses and Centres for Spiritual Renewal been so full as they are in the 1990s. Apart from the traditional silent retreats, a whole range of themes is on offer – healing, painting, music, poetry, gardening. There are opportunities for whole families to stay; and there are individually guided retreats for anything from one to thirty days. With such a wide variety available, it is hardly surprising that not only are these places attracting more church members, but are themselves becoming centres of evangelism by welcoming those who don't belong to any church at all.

Prayer and the Holy Spirit

How then do we become a praying church? Renewal happens when the members of a local church stop regarding prayer as the spiritual quotation marks at the beginning and end of a meeting or as the safe liturgical words which can be said in church without too much personal involvement. Jesus taught his disciples only one prayer. Luke even hints that the disciples may have had to insist that he taught them even that, on the grounds that John the Baptist had taught his followers a prayer so they ought to have one too! But prayer is not primarily about words. It is about the search, sometimes the struggle, to be at one with God. Paul writes:

> We do not know how we ought to pray; the Spirit himself pleads with God for us in groans that words cannot express.

And God, who sees into our hearts, knows what the thought of the Spirit is; because the Spirit pleads with God on behalf of his people and in accordance with his will.

(Romans 8:26–7)

God's Mission – Not Ours

The more prayerful and open to the Holy Spirit we are, the more we come to realise that the mission in which we are engaged does not depend on us but on God. We do well to remember in this Decade of Evangelism a British lay monk called Pelagius, who lived in the fifth century. He was condemned by the Church for heresy, because he held that it is we ourselves who take the first and fundamental steps towards salvation by our own efforts. It is a heresy which still tempts. But this is God's mission not ours. Renewal will come not because of what we do ourselves. It will come through the prayerful opening of our hearts to the renewing power of his Holy Spirit.

A New Vision

Never before has the Church of England made such a concerted attempt to deepen its prayer life and fire its witness. But there are still many Christians today who stand on the edge of the Decade of Evangelism, confused, fearful and hesitant. They are regular worshippers, members of church councils who could and should be the forefront missionaries of their Church. The churches they belong to wait to be released to become the vibrant centres of good news that they could and should be. The Holy Spirit is still waiting, longing, to fill them with his renewing love and power and use them to transform the lives of men, women and children everywhere. May this be the prayer of every church and every Christian:

Father pour out your Spirit upon us and grant us
A new vision of your glory, a new experience of your power
A new faithfulness to your word, and a new consecration to
  your service
That your love may grow among us and your kingdom come
Through Jesus Christ our Lord. Amen.

3

Equipping

Every Member Ministry

A church I visited in the United States had a memorable notice-board outside which read: 'Ministers – every member of this church'. That vision has already been spelt out by the ecumenical church leaders in England when they spoke of the responsibility of every Christian to pass on the good news of Jesus. Not all church members will want to see that as their duty; others, while recognising that they ought to, will dread becoming involved in such a ministry. That means that not only equipping, but also motivating, every member of every church to live and share the Gospel is a top priority for this Decade.

The Roman Catholic leader, Cardinal Suenens, has said that a Christian is not a Christian unless he or she is actively seeking to make other people Christians. A statement from the Orthodox Church claims: 'We do not have the option of keeping the good news to ourselves . . . the uncommunicated gospel is a patent contradiction.' From the World Council of Churches come these vivid words: 'The Gospel is like manna. It cannot be kept. If we do not share it, we lose it. If we do not use it, it goes stale. It has been given to us, like bread, for our daily use.' Somewhat in contrast comes a classic piece of English understatement from a 1992 editorial in the journal *Theology*: 'Evangelism, passing on the message of Jesus, cannot be objected to among Christians'!

Seeing every Christian as an agent of mission does not mean that every Christian is expected to become a mini-Billy Graham – though praise God for all this evangelistic gifts which have brought so many to Christ. Ephesians 4:11 makes it very clear that only some people are called specifically to be evangelists, but we are all called to be witnesses to our faith in ways that match the individual and varied gifts that everyone has been given by God. The greatest gift is the grace and capacity to be like Jesus.

Charged with Divine Electricity

How did Jesus set about equipping his disciples for his mission? First he spent the whole night in prayer. Then he chose them. When the present Decade of Evangelism was launched with prayer, the key people were in place already, and contrary to a lot of popular opinion, the churches of our different denominations are in a potentially strong position. In the United Kingdom there is one ordained minister for every 1,200 people. By European standards this is a big army of leaders and trainers: on the continent there is only one ordained minister for every 2,500 people. Even taking into account the recent decline in the numbers being ordained, there are still six clergy to every four GPs in this country. The clergy remain an important part of the social fabric of our society and, for the most part, are effectively positioned for evangelism.

More significant still is the strength of the laity, the forefront missionaries of the Church. There are around 50,000 Christian congregations in the United Kingdom. No other organisation has so many active members so strategically positioned. The structures and the people are in place; it is a question of opening them to the Holy Spirit to equip and release them, so that every congregation may again become the dynamic missionary presence the Christian Church was at the start, and was always meant to be. As the great Baptist, Charles Spurgeon, often told his students:

Great things are done by the Holy Spirit when a whole church is roused to sacred energy . . . It should be an ambition, in the power of the Holy Spirit, to work the entire Church into a fine missionary condition . . . charged to the full with divine electricity . . . so that whoever comes into contact with it shall feel its power.

Learn by Taking Risks

Jesus taught his disciples in parables and riddles. He was forever probing, exploring, questioning, and provoking. They never knew what to expect next, especially when he sent them out still relatively untrained. The twelve disciples (Matthew 6) and the seventy-two (Luke 10) learned how to evangelise by doing it.

The best way to prepare a Church for evangelism is by being evangelistic. It is sometimes argued that, before going out to pass on the good news, the faithful must first be specially taught what to say and do. The surest way to strengthen the faithful is to entrust them with an immediate missionary task so that the training and the exercise go hand in hand. Jesus took the risk of sending his disciples out and God is ready to do the same now in sending out the disciples of this generation. In a recent sermon, Archbishop Desmond Tutu expressed it thus: 'Our God is a God of risks. God is ready to jeopardise His divine enterprise, to have me as his agent of transformation so that the Kingdom of this world will become the Kingdom of God and His Christ.'

In Luke 12:11–12 Jesus assures those who take the risk for him that if they get into difficulty: 'Do not be worried about how you will defend yourself or what you will say. For the Holy Spirit will teach you at that time what you should say.' There are plenty of examples in the history of God's Church of apparently ill-equipped Christians going out on their mission in the name of Christ and finding the Holy Spirit empowering them with what to say. In living and sharing the Gospel with others they themselves found the Lord in a new and living way.

It is better for us to learn and grow in our faith in the context of those who do not share it than be taught it in the safe confines of the cocooned atmosphere of the Church. All too often the detailed Church training programmes can be an excuse for not taking up the real challenge to engage with the world.

Opportunists for Christ

At the Ascension Jesus left his still bemused and ill-equipped apostles to get on with God's mission. According to Matthew 28:19–20 he gave them his Great Commission:

> Go, then, to all peoples everywhere and make them my disciples: baptise them in the name of the Father, the Son and the Holy Spirit, and teach them to obey everything I have commanded you. And I will be with you always, to the end of the age.

It is too easy to dismiss these words as not being the words of Jesus. The Trinitarian formula clearly belongs to the early Church rather than Jesus. But the verses are an authentic summary of Jesus' wish, evident at the end of all four gospels and in the mission of the twelve and the seventy-two, that his followers should go out.

The meaning of this commission is not about contriving special campaigns in order to convey the Gospel message. It is about grasping the natural opportunities as they arise on life's journey. This is the Emmaus Road principle of evangelism – taking up the chances to be alongside people. Jesus, we are told, talked 'together with them' on the road, not at them, and the truth dawned. We are called to be opportunists for Christ.

In terms of this decade that means realising the evangelistic potential of the moments that matter in people's lives – the births, the deaths, the sorrows, the joys; using community events at Christmas and Easter, Remembrance Sunday, civic services as times to build up trust in the Pauline sense of being all things to all men that they may be won for Christ; and, where there are schools, taking every opportunity as parents, governors, staff, clergy and pupils to witness to the good news of Jesus.

All Things to All People

In his first letter to the Corinthian Church, Paul spelt out some principles of evangelism, emphasising the importance of being equipped to communicate the things of God by being on the same wavelength as those we are with. 'I am a free man, nobody's slave; but I make myself everybody's slave in order to win as many people as possible.' He went on to clarify what that meant. When he was working with Jews he lived as if he himself were still a Jew under the Mosaic Law in order to win them for Christ. When working with gentiles, he lived like a gentile, outside the Jewish Law, in order to win them.

> Among the weak in faith I become weak like one of them, in order to win them. So I become all things to all men, that I may save of them by whatever means are possible. All this I do for the gospel's sake, in order to share its blessings.
>
> (1 Corinthians 9:19–23)

Love One Another

The Great Commission also makes clear that passing on the good news is to lead to enlisting people into Christian fellowship. They are to become disciples, incorporated by baptism into the Church, but that is not all. There is a further point, which is crucial to a full understanding of the nature of Christian evangelism. Jesus is quoted as saying, 'Teach them to obey everything I have commanded you'. The task at the beginning of the first decade of evangelism, as described in Matthew 28:19–20, is not only about inviting people to accept Jesus as

Lord and be baptised, but simultaneously teaching them to
obey his new command, given in John 13:34–5, to: 'Love one
another. As I have loved you, so must you love one another.
If you love one another, then everyone will know you are my
disciples.' At the heart of the Great Commission is the injunc-
tion to love. It is a constantly recurring theme through all
evangelism – that what we are and how we act speaks more
powerfully than anything we say.

The Living Christ

The point is encapsulated in a poem of unknown authorship
called *The Living Christ*:

Not merely in the words you say, not only in the deeds
   confessed,
But in the most unconscious way is Christ expressed.
Is it a very saintly smile? A holy light upon your brow?
Oh no! I felt his presence while you laughed just now.
For me, 'twas not the truth you taught, to you so clear, to
   me so dim:
But when you came, you straightway brought a sense of him.
So from your life he beckons me, and from your heart his
   love is shed.
Till I lose sight of you, and see the Christ instead.

We are to attract people by what we are, 'as we try to look
with the eyes of Christ – into the eyes of Christ in the other
person'. The purpose is to attract them, not to us, but to God
in Christ. 'For it is not ourselves that we preach; we preach
Jesus Christ as Lord and ourselves as your servants for Jesus'
sake' (2 Corinthians 4:5).

We Cannot Help It

The story of the early Church is not of disciples putting on special courses in evangelistic techniques. It is the story of what happened when groups of Christians stayed together in fellowship, eating and praying and hearing about Jesus. It is the story of how the Holy Spirit equipped the disciples, transforming them, so that with zest and energy they went out to witness to their faith in Jesus. When challenged, Peter and John summed up why they did it: 'We cannot help speaking about what we ourselves have seen and heard' (Acts 4:20).

Recent studies have shown that most people who come to explore the Christian faith do so through conversations with their friends or within their families, rather than through great evangelistic events. Very often the most effective way of introducing someone to the Christian faith is by telling them, in an unselfconscious way at a natural moment, the story of our own journey – a journey which is always incomplete.

One thing that encourages me at Confirmation services is the readiness with which adult candidates talk about their preparation classes and the freedom they found there to share their experiences and doubts and faith. I have been told this so many times that I am persuaded that chatting about how the facts of faith relate to the experiences of life is not so big a problem as some fear it is. The natural unselfconscious testimony of the ordinary Christian in the world is worth countless sermons in church. With the enabling power of the Holy Spirit, that is proving to be the most strategically effective way of bringing people to Christ. I am coming across more Christians who, like Peter and John, cannot help 'gossiping the gospel' – telling what they have seen and heard.

Resources Available

Although being motivated for mission is more important than learning techniques, more teaching about the faith can itself often be a motivating force. The lack of confidence of many Christians about their faith is one of the main obstacles to evangelism. Since the launch of the Decade almost every diocese has put on courses and conferences to help congregations to deepen their faith and heighten their awareness of the need for personal witness, in accordance with individual gifts and circumstances. The response to these has often been exceptional. Reports have come in of many major events aimed at motivating the laity for their missionary task – many of them attended by a thousand people at a time.

Some imaginative material has also been produced to help equip Christians to pass on their faith. The *Before We Go* course, which comes from an Anglo-Catholic stable, has now been used by more than 40,000 people. One of the largest lay groups within the Church of England, the Mothers' Union, is using its *I Believe and Trust* to great effect. Because the Mothers' Union, which in many parts of the world is a very significant evangelistic body, has branches in many parishes of the Church of England, its course could have considerable influence on parish strategies for mission.

Springboard

As the crescendo now builds up, the Archbishops of Canterbury and York have appointed Bishop Michael Marshall and Canon Michael Green to lead their *Springboard* initiative. This is part of a long-term strategy agreed in the first months of the Decade when, with the backing of the Steering Group and the Board of Mission, the Archbishops first approached 'the two Michaels'. They have strong and proven evangelistic gifts. Their diary for visits around the country to help unlock the potential and increase the effectiveness of congregations is very well filled. The Archbishops have stated that the aim is to help 'the Church reach out with the good news of the Gospel to the unbelieving, the lapsed, lukewarm, disillusioned and down-hearted in their communities'.

Friendship Evangelism

Whilst *Springboard* will focus on major events and training conferences, a more low-key approach is provided by a new video course in 'friendship evangelism' produced by Anglican Renewal Ministries. This is presented by the popular and gifted evangelist J John. Suitable for groups, families or individuals, one of its practical suggestions is to follow the widely used 'Singapore 5–3–1' method. The idea is to pray regularly for one year for five friends who have not yet made a Christian commitment. Pray that before the twelve months are up you will have had the chance to speak to at least three of them about the good news of Jesus. Pray that by the end of the year at least one of them has become a Christian. As J John points out, if everyone did this successfully every church congregation would double in size each year.

Equipping the Baptised

Many baptised members of the Church still do not see themselves as the people best placed to be the ones to pass on the Gospel. If they do, they sometimes receive little help. In *The Laity Today and Tomorrow* Edmund Flood wrote:

> I am now a sales manager of a major steel company. In the almost thirty years of my professional career, my church has never once suggested that there be any other type of accounting of my on-the-job ministry to others. My church has never once offered to improve those skills which could make me a better minister, nor has it ever asked if I needed any kind of support in what I was doing.
>
> There was never an inquiry into the types of ethical decisions I must face, or whether I seek to communicate the faith to my co-workers. I have never been in a congregation where there was any type of public affirmation of a ministry in my career. In short, I must conclude that my church does

not have the least interest whether or how I minister in my daily work.

Quoting this extract in a recent lecture, Margaret Selby, Sheffield Diocese Deputy Director of Ministry, pleaded for space in local church life for people to be allowed to see their work as of prime importance. 'My own experience', she said, 'has been of a parish where all church activities were cancelled except for the Eucharist, to free the people for real engagement with the world.'

That engagement is spelt out at the baptism of every new Christian. It happens near the moment when the cross, which we all wear from the day of our baptism, is signed on our foreheads with these words:

I sign you with the cross, the sign of Christ.
Do not be ashamed to confess the faith of Christ crucified.
Fight valiantly under the banner of Christ against sin, the
    world and the devil,
And continue his faithful soldier and servant to the end of
    your life.

The fact that these things are the responsibility of all baptised Christians and not just those who are keen on evangelism is being reflected in the fact that the vision for the Decade of Evangelism is being taken into every part of the Church's life. A liturgical group is examining evangelism and worship; a Local Ordained Ministry course is teaching its students to think through evangelism theologically and practically; several cathedrals have organised evangelistic and teaching events; a diocesan Board of Education is producing a major study on education and evangelism. A particularly significant move has been the introduction of the theology and practice of evangelism into the training of Readers, and post-ordination and in-service training of the clergy now includes the equipping of the laity for their missionary role.

Love and Joy

Like so much of the Decade of Evangelism, all this seems very
'churchy'. Courses and projects are important, and when they
are imaginative they can alter outlooks and give church life
some much-needed zip, but the greatest resource is within
ourselves. We all blossom when someone recognises the good
in is and encourages us to give of our best: many of us know
how easily we can lose confidence and shrivel up when we are
constantly criticised and told we are not doing well. Archbishop
Desmond Tutu made this point in a memorable sermon:

> We are sure to break that special cup of the lady who is
> always fussy about her precious heirlooms. We become all
> thumbs in her presence. Just notice how Jesus was able to
> get a prostitute like Mary Magdalene to become one of the
> greatest saints. He mentioned the quality in her which
> nobody else had noticed – her great capacity to love; and
> from selling her body she became one of his most loyal
> followers.

The way forward for making every Christian an agent of
mission is for us to start noticing in one another, and in ourselves, the capacity to love. That is the key piece of equipment
for living and sharing the Gospel. I am not sure it is achieved
primarily with tapes and videos. It is more to do with our inner
relationship with God, and knowing and feeling that, in spite
of everything, he loves us and his love never fails. 'We love
him because he first loved us' (1 John 4:19). That knowledge
brings a deep sense of joy. You cannot try to be joyful: it just
happens. When the truth becomes clear, joy is spontaneous.

As the Orthodox Archbishop Metropolitan Anthony Bloom
once said about living and sharing the Gospel: 'If you have
discovered joy, how can you not give joy to others? If truly
you have come nearer the truth, how can you keep it to yourself? Go into the world with a radiance, with a joy, with an
intensity that will make everyone say: You have something you

never had before and which I do not have. Where can I get it?'

4

Exploring

Other Faiths

The Roman Catholic theologian Hans Kung has said: 'There can be no peace in the world without peace between the religions of the world. There can be no peace between the religions of the world without dialogue between the people of the world's religions. There can be no dialogue between the people of the world's religions without theological research.' The Anglican Consultative Council has warned: 'The increase of militant fundamentalism in the three great monotheistic religions (Christianity, Judaism and Islam) is at best unhelpful and at worst life-threatening. We commend to the international Christian community the importance of fellowship, friendship and dialogue with people of other faiths.'

The position of the Anglican Communion on other faiths was outlined at the same Lambeth Conference which called for the Decade of Evangelism. The bishops commended dialogue with other faiths as part of Christian discipleship and mission; and, as the Anglican Consultative Council went on to say in 1990: 'In all our efforts in dialogue we cannot lay aside the truth that God in Christ has been present and active in all nations, cultures and religions, nor can we lay aside our call to be fishers of women and men . . . This dialogue may require a change within Christians as well, not in terms of their relationship with Christ, but in their understanding of dogma, tradition and church paraphernalia which may be confused by them with the truths of the faith.'

Assurances Given

Unfortunately, but not surprisingly, the launch of the Decade of Evangelism has led leaders of other faiths in England to express deep suspicions about its aims. One of the earliest letters I received at the Steering Group was from the Council for Christians and Jews asking for assurance that there were no plans to target Jews. I was able to give that assurance, but the Jewish community, which does not itself believe in seeking converts, remains concerned. The Chief Rabbi, Dr Jonathan Sachs, has responded by calling for a Decade of Renewal among Jews.

The real issue is how Christians are to communicate effectively and sensitively with their Jewish neighbours that the New Testament is the fulfilment of all the prophets dreamed, and that the Messiah has come. In making that point, Michael Lawson, a Jew 'converted' to Christianity, adds that the challenge is to do this in such a sympathetic way that Jewish hearers do not feel got at, and aggressively hunted down. It is the manner of evangelism not permission for evangelism which is the difficulty. Emphasising the fact that it was love which motivated God to send his Son, and Jesus to send out his followers first to the Jews then to all nations, he stresses that, if it is good news we want to bring them, then the great need is for Jews to be loved and befriended by Christians. Such love is a divine ethic, far more effective than targeting, and far more likely to give dialogue a chance.

Christian–Muslim Dialogue

Concern about the Decade has also been expressed by Muslim leaders, and assurances have been given to them also that there are no plans to target their communities. Suspicions, however, remain. A Decade of Islamic Revivalism has been initiated by Dr Zaki Badawi, a leading Muslim moderate, who explained that it is a response to, as well as a gesture of collaboration with, the Decade of Evangelism. It is also designed to allay fears among the many different 'denominations' within the Muslim community in England who see the Decade as a Christian threat. The editor of the *Muslim News* appealed: 'Faith communities would be better off working together for spiritual renewal in Britain and aiming for common goals, such as the legislative protection of those individuals who identify themselves by their religious beliefs.'

It is hardly surprising that communities of other faiths who are still learning to grapple with issues like employment, education and the maintenance of their traditional patterns of community and family life in an alien culture are worried about the implications of a Decade of Evangelism. Their worry is shared by quite a number of Christians who fear that the Decade will encourage further the already disturbing rise in religious fundamentalism.

Nevertheless, as Andrew Wingate shows in his book about Muslim–Christian dialogue in practice, *Encounter in the Spirit*, Muslims and Christians have in fact been engaging in dialogue for several years. He tells of such a group in Birmingham whose members have not changed their faiths but have grown in community and understanding. Perhaps the most valuable result of such meetings is not what happens in the group itself but the 'ripple effect' of going back into the separate communities to witness to the fact that, 'Muslims or Christians are not all like this or that'. Such meetings are encounters in the Spirit. Andrew Wingate writes:

> We, as Christians, do not own the Spirit. The Spirit is the enabler of all that is happening between us – leading us into all truth, breaking down the barriers between us, creating out of a dialogue between two parties a common search together for the truth that sets us free . . . I hope this book may encourage Christians and Muslims, wherever they are, to work with each other and not against each other, and indeed with people of all faiths and none, to realise that better life, particularly for the poor amongst them, who are

the special concern of the scriptures of both faiths, and of
the teaching of both Jesus and Muhammad.

Size of Communities

No accurate information is currently available in this country
about the population of other faiths. Until the post-war years
the main one was the Jewish community. Today, it is estimated
that those who belong to other faiths number no more than
4.5% of the population, i.e. 2.5 million. About one million of
those are Muslims. The rest are made up from 400,000 Hindus,
400,000 Sikhs, 300,000 Jews and about 100,000 Chinese, some
of them Buddhist. There are other small religious groups too.
Nor must we forget, though they are not included in these
statistics, the 35,000 Asian and Indian Christians. The concen-
tration of the 2.5 million is mainly in London and in major
conurbations of the Midlands and North. My own diocese of
Wakefield contains Europe's largest Muslim training centre;
and some of our church schools have over 80% Asian children.
A new mosque is being built next door to a church school in
Wakefield. It is said that, within forty years, one third of the
population of the Bradford Metropolitan District which edges
on Wakefield is likely to be of other faiths.

Confrontation Counterproductive

The issue of the relationship between the Decade of Evangelism and other faiths is therefore a live issue. It was given a
heightened profile by the *Open Letter to the Leadership of the
Church of England* which was signed by a large number of
mainly, but not entirely, evangelical clergy. They expressed
concern that the Gospel should be clearly presented in this
decade.

    We desire to love and respect people of other faiths. We

acknowledge and respect their rights and freedoms. We wholeheartedly support co-operation in appropriate community, social, moral and political issues between Christians and those of other faiths wherever this is possible. Nevertheless, we believe it to be our Lord's command that his Gospel be clearly proclaimed, openly and sensitively, to all people (including those of other faiths) with the intention that they should come to faith in him for salvation.

Christians do have a Gospel to proclaim – but how can that be done without denigrating other faiths? As the Archbishop of Canterbury has said:

We should respect the integrity of other faiths while proclaiming and acting out our own firm belief in Jesus Christ as our Lord. Deliberate confrontation with other faiths would be counterproductive and divisive. A predominantly Christian society nurtures tolerance and constructive relationship with minority faiths; and the Christian Churches need to work with people of other faiths in combating the shallow materialism of much contemporary life. We must never hide our beliefs; nor would other faiths respect us if we did. But our mission is to society as a whole, to all who have ears to hear, and especially to those who are half-hearted in their Christian commitment or have lost their faith altogether. Friction with minority faiths is an unprotected distraction from the enormous positive agenda of the Decade.

Christianity a Public Truth

Dr Christopher Lamb of the Church of England's Board of Mission puts the point like this: 'If we are to be faithful to our understanding of the finality of Christ . . . we have to make it plain, as it is not at present, that the Christian faith is for all people because it is public truth.' In other words, though we are required to engage with and try to understand members of other faiths, that does not in any sense imply a capitulation to other faiths.

Uniqueness of Christ

Few issues relating to the Decade are being discussed more keenly than the relationship between Christianity and other faiths. There seem to be three main positions. First there are those who hold firmly to the uniqueness and finality of Jesus Christ. They say that an explicit confession of Jesus as Lord is necessary for salvation. This is known as the exclusivist position. The second position, called inclusivist, also says that God was shown supremely in Christ, but also point to the power and presence of God in other religions and in all creation. The third position is pluralism. The recent General Synod report, *Multi-Faith Worship?* describes this as seeing the differences between religions 'as arising from the different human interpretations of the revelation of the one God according to cultural limitations, and this may (but need not necessarily) involve a belief that all religions are on a similar level in relation to ultimate truth'.

The problem of regarding the three position in isolation is illustrated by one of the leading thinkers in the whole area of the relationship of the Gospel and pluralist society, Bishop Lesslie Newbigin whom the report quotes. He describes his position as:

> . . . exclusivist in the sense that it affirms the unique truth of the revelation in Jesus Christ, but it is not exclusivist in the sense of denying the possibility of the salvation of the non-Christian. It is inclusivist in the sense that it refuses to limit the saving grace of God to the members of the Christian Church, but it rejects the inclusivism which regards the non-Christian religions as vehicles of salvation. It is pluralist in the sense of acknowledging the gracious work of God in the lives of all human beings, but it rejects a pluralism which

denies the uniqueness and decisiveness of what God has done
in Jesus Christ.

God in Other Faiths

The truth is that there is no consensus on this central issue of
the place of Jesus Christ in relation to other faiths. It is of
crucial importance for the exploring of our own faith in this
Decade of Evangelism that a consensus is achieved. The Archbishop of Canterbury's own contributions to the debate are
bound to be significant. He has already made it clear that he
accepts that God is not absent from other faiths, and indeed,
that other faiths can echo truths to be found in the Christian
faith. The Archbishop has also said that he accepts there can
be, and often are, 'grace-filled moments in the lives of non-
Christians through which the one God speaks authentically and
really'. He is equally clear in stating that he cannot accept that
the claims and the contribution of Christ are 'negotiable'.

Gospel and Culture

Much work has been done in recent years on the relationship
between the Gospel and the culture within which we live. The
Church itself is a society with its own language and culture,
and the faith it stands for needs to be made known in varied
cultural forms. The Lambeth bishops stressed the urgent need
to find new entry points into secular Western culture, and
especially youth culture, in order that the Church might engage
in dialogue with the world of which it is a part.

In 1991 the Church of England's Board of Mission produced
a significant report *Good News in Our Times – the Gospel and
Our Contemporary Cultures* which attempted to set an agenda
for action and reflection in these areas during the Decade and
beyond. The report highlights the two major differences in
approach to the whole subject. At one end of the spectrum are

those who believe that the good news of the Gospel can be formulated in a single group of statements that can then be simply communicated in every context and culture. At the other end are those who emphasise the need to discover what God is doing and saying in the world and so identify what is the Good News for each individual and group.

Dialogue Essential

The authors of *Good News in Our Times*, who themselves represented a wide range of opinion, agreed that the good news is not 'a single, unchanging package that simply has to be unwrapped'. On the other hand it recognised 'that the focus of the Gospel is the story of the birth, death, resurrection and ascension of Jesus Christ and that each community and every individual has to be helped to discover what is Good News for them by linking their story to his story'. The report ends with a call to Christians to be willing to cross cultural boundaries in order to listen and to enter into a genuine dialogue with others, to give a continuing and quiet witness until genuine opportunities for sharing faith are given, and to tackle the immense task of bringing to bear the Gospel message on the whole of modern culture.

Secular England?

In England only 14% of all children are said to have any contact with a church: most parents and grandparents have none. But still within living memory is the time when the Christian faith was overtly part of our culture. Sunday Schools were well-attended and most children knew at least some Bible stories. In church and state schools many teachers, even if they did not claim to be practising Christians, had a Christian background and affirmed behaviour in accordance with Christian ideals. In just two generations that seems to have been lost. In an age of videos, Bible stories are no longer part of the common currency of our culture. The child who does go to church may face ridicule among his or her peers.

It is tempting to contrast this seemingly bleak picture with stories that have emerged, for example, from Eastern Europe. There are moving accounts of how, in the face of arbitrary persecution and chronic hardship, ordinary people have kept the faith and made sure it has been handed on. As barriers came down, churches were full and their leaders often played major roles in forming the new democracies. Few who saw it will forget the large cross carried by a group of young people in the milling crowd outside the Russian parliament building in the turbulent days of the attempted 1991 coup.

But the contrast between the two pictures is not as clear as at first it might seem. In Eastern Europe, Christianity is having to face the tide of secularism which has come in the wake of freedom from ideology. In England claims about the level of secularism need to be questioned. Secularism is the belief that everyday life has no relationship whatsoever with the divine. Can it really be said in the 1990s that England is a secular society?

Recent surveys indicate that, discounting those who attend a Christian church regularly and those who belong to another faith, 60% of the population still claim some kind of allegiance to Christianity. Around 25% claim to be agnostic or atheist. In other words, the Church has the immediate task of spreading the good news to around 85% of the nation – most of whom already feel they have some, albeit tenuous, link with the Church. A census was taken of all congregations on one Sunday in 1989: 10% of the adult population was in church, and ten years earlier it had been 11%. Most of that 1% decline had occurred between 1979 and 1985. Those figures do not represent the major decline that has been mentioned regularly in the media: we are not yet a secular society.

In a recent interview on the subject, the Archbishop of Canterbury said:

I don't criticise our society for being too secular. Secular means absence of God. The majority of people believe in God and most people pray, so that in most people there is a moral sense, a moral awareness. They know what is right and what is wrong, and that is why when you face them with these things they instinctively know . . . The problem is our scientific and technological culture. We are influenced by that culture which has become materialistic – but not necessarily secular.

A fascinating statistic about the early 1990s is the fact that Stephen Hawking's book, *A Brief History of Time* has beaten all records in its number of weeks on the bestseller lists. That it may not have been read by everyone who has bought it is less significant than the indication the purchase itself gives about the curiosity our generation has about deep questions. Hawking's book is not just about the law of physics. He makes it clear that his ultimate aim is to explain 'why it is that we and the universe exist . . . If we find the answer to that, it would be the ultimate triumph of human reason – for then we would know the mind of God'.

As *The Times* noted, if Hawking's book has a direct precedent in the bestseller business, it is probably Bishop John Robinson's *Honest to God* – and the record-breaking sales of those two books 'hardly support the argument that the British are not interested in the study of first or last things'.

5

Changing

The Credibility Gap

The issue that the Churches must face up to in this decade is not so much that people do not believe in God, but that they do not find the Churches credible. Current surveys consistently indicate a high rate of belief in God, but the difficulty is in converting that often confused belief into committed faith. Jack Dominian, observing that science and technology have transformed mankind's view of reality, noted recently that 'the West, which still looks at the world as a mystery and still thinks God is probable, is not impressed by the God that the Churches project'.

Psychology, sociology and genetic understanding of personality have all advanced considerably over the past one hundred years. This has helped people to understand more about their own incompleteness, imperfections and the limitations of social order. The result is that sin is seen as having far more to do with the limitations imposed by personal character and environment. Jack Dominian argues that evangelists should therefore bring to the fore the kingdom of God, preached in terms of social justice, peace and love, rather than stressing personal guilt: 'Evangelism needs to emphasise the changes that Christianity has to effect within itself before it can commend itself to the outside world.'

Home and Family

The place where the facts of faith and the reality of life are most likely to meet and make some sense is not in the church, but at home. The dull routine of daily living can be an extra-ordinary communion with God, for the home has its own lit-urgical cycle through everyday activity. Jack Dominian has considerable experience in the field of marriage and in an article entitled *Evangelism Begins at Home* he writes:

> If in this Decade of Evangelism all the Churches can recog-nise the importance of marriage, then a breakthrough will be made in making the Christian faith come alive . . . What happens . . . in the home is the principal way that the majority of people grasp the centrality of God in their lives.

Linking the vision of love in the home with the reality of God, he pleads for a change in Church structures which would place marriage and the family much more squarely on the map. There is plenty of evidence to show the pressures on home and family life in this decade. One in every three people is single: either unmarried, separated, divorced or widowed. Faced with that situation, a Church which wants to be evangelistic must devote time and energy to marriage preparation, to continuing to support couples throughout their marriages, to assisting the separated and divorced, and to affirming the unmarried and widowed. This is essential if the Decade is to see the Church becoming a community of love which radiates love.

Church Schools

One of the more imaginative documents to emerge through the General Synod since the start of the Decade has been *All God's Children?*. This well-received ecumenical report argues that the Church must change its priorities if it is to communicate the gospel to the millions of children who face adult life without any awareness of a God who loves them. It calls for the Church to take a much more positive role and to develop a radical new strategy for children's work and evangelism, remembering that people's hearts and minds are moulded early in life.

There are well over 4,000 Church of England primary schools in the country, providing the Church with privileged access and influence. In addition there are many other schools, both state and independent, which have warm and close links with their local church. One of the main recommendations of *All God's Children?* is to encourage local Christians to support the work of Christian witness and the promotion of spiritual development of pupils in schools by teachers, governors, parents and others. Our church schools provide us with golden opportunities to educate the young in the principles of love, which will colour their relationships with each other, and their understanding of God's love for them through Jesus.

School Mission Statements

The new Schools Act and the Decade of Evangelism are a twin incentive to all concerned with our local church schools to overhaul policies and procedures for educating children in this way. It will require imagination and integrity. There have also been suggestions that every church school should have its own 'Mission Statement'. This would set out the school's aims in such a way as to show how what happens there will witness to the Gospel. The idea is that admissions, curriculum, provision for special needs, staff appointments, relationships, collective worship and religious education, should be consistent with the aims set out publicly in the 'Mission Statement'.

In their booklet, *Looking for Quality in a Church School*, the Church of England Board of Education and the National Society go to some length to emphasise that a church school, because of its foundation, is different from other schools. It will have a theological understanding about its existence and purpose which cannot be present in quite the same explicit way in a school which does not have a Christian foundation.

Teachers, Parents, Governors – Forefront Missionaries

It follows from all this that the influence of teachers and parents who are Christians is a very important factor in the life and well-being of the church school. The responsibility and power of governors is also considerable. They are all forefront missionaries operating in a vitally important missionary setting. Great care should be taken to make sure that governors of church schools have a commitment to Christian witness and the spiritual development of the pupils. This is a vital evangelistic responsibility which, when exercised with wisdom and sensitivity, can have a positive and lasting Christian influence on the lives of those who pass through the school.

Governors are advised to be clear what they expect in terms of faith commitment from staff. While there is room in church schools for good teachers without religious commitment, it is undesirable to appoint staff who cannot, in conscience, support the school's overtly religious aims and practices.

Governors of church schools also have the opportunity to see that religious education and collective worship are taken seriously and done well. These are areas in which church schools especially should excel. The collective worship, while interesting all members of the school community, should draw regularly from the Anglican tradition, and a wealth of excellent resource material is available. This remains true for schools where, as in my own diocese, there is a predominantly Muslim attendance, along with Sikhs and Hindus. The other faith communities expect a Church of England school to be sensitive to their existence but overtly Christian. They prefer to send their children to a school where faith is seen to be important.

Contact With the Young

The ability of the Church to relate to the young has a direct bearing on not only its present but also its future health. The American Sociological Review carried an interesting report, based on work done by the National Opinion Research Centre in sixteen countries, including the United Kingdom. It showed that, from the proportion of the population attending Church aged under twenty-five years, it is possible to predict precisely the proportion who will be attending Church in their mid-forties and fifties. In other words, the fewer young people who attend church now, the fewer adults there will be in Church in thirty years' time. The research showed that this link appears to be far more significant than any other single factor – including the conversion of people to the faith in adult life. Contact with young people is therefore absolutely essential for the continuing life of the Church.

The Importance of Worship

It should now be clear that the main forum for change in this decade should be those places where individuals spend most of their time, such as the home and the school. But, if that change is to happen and new points of entry found for the Gospel to reach into homes and schools, the attitudes of the people in the local church and the emphases of local church policy may also have to change. Mother Teresa was once asked by an interviewer about her vocation caring for the poor on the streets of Delhi. Her reply was that her vocation was not to care for the poor but to worship God. Everything flowed from that. Her work, for which she is famed, begins each day only after many hours of prayer in the chapel.

The Archbishops' Commission on Music's report, *In Tune with Heaven* makes the same point:

> Giving glory to God is not just one, or even the first, of a long string of reasons. It is the fundamental, deepest and truest reason, all-sufficient in itself. All the other reasons that are given for worship are to be seen, not as products of our own contriving, but as the gifts of God in return for our response of giving him the glory.

Worship is, and always must be, at the heart of all that the Decade of Evangelism is about. The hope is that more people will be drawn to worship God, so it is important that our public worship should take account of the needs and contexts of those who do not normally attend. Worship should be a pathway to God for those who are strangers to the Church as well as for regular members. Alas, the experience of some who do venture into church is not encouraging. This is an extract from a letter I received from Jane from West Sussex:

> I feel very disenchanted by the majority of churches in my area and wonder what can be done. I am, like many young people in their mid-twenties, a third generation of non-churchgoers. I have spent the entirety of my youth with nobody to talk to about Christianity and the multitude of questions I wished to ask. About a year ago now, I finally ventured into a local church and found the services so full of pomp I was completely confused. After months of shopping around I found a church which was better, but I still feel the services are not catering for people such as myself. What I am trying to say is that I feel there are thousands of people like myself, brought up outside a Christian background who do not know where to start.

Communicating in Ways That Make Sense

An encouraging number of churches have risen to challenges such as Jane's. The Mustard Seed Church in Slough is a good example of how barriers can be brought down by a down-to-earth style and a genuine involvement in local issues. The prayerful thinking behind what happens there is that the Church must, as a priority, reach out to the unchurched nominal Christians, and the non-Christians too, with the good news of Jesus. To do this it must build bridges and speak in a language and style which is appropriate to where the unchurched and the non-Christians are. As Pat Thomas, the minister, says:

Many people don't have books in their homes, and yet we expect them to come to church where we immediately present them with a pile of books full of meaningless phrases. How do you connect with people who have been unemployed or whose homes have been repossessed? Do we expect people on the edge to come to our posh churches? What is mission here? How is the gospel lived and communicated?

What is sometimes forgotten is that many such people are, in fact, members of the Church already. Communicating is just as much of a problem for them – and indeed for many more church members than most church leaders seem to realise. I remember attending a Parochial Church Council when the Decade of Evangelism was being explained. 'What's he talking about?' was the response of the man next to me, who then gave up listening and read his copy of *The Sun* instead.

I did not blame him. The very word 'evangelism' gets us off to a wrong start. It is an abstract noun; it is apparently a fact that the higher their intellectual level, the more people use abstract nouns. But a decade of evangelism is about 'every member' ministry and mission. It is about real people, *Sun* readers, all of them passing on the good news of Jesus. It's either that or it's dead.

For most people (including many with A levels and degrees, PGCEs and Diplomas), it is better to say 'Ivanisevic hits the ball hard' than 'Ivanisevic has a lot of racket power'. It is more direct. It says what it means. It appeals to a wider range of people. Whenever we use an abstract noun it distances most people from what it means. Concrete expressions and active verbs are what make most people sit up and take notice.

I Didn't Feel Welcome

When I was away recently I attended a service in a cathedral. The music and the building were lovely; the congregation looked miserable. I sat among them in my holiday clothes. No-one spoke to me. No-one smiled at me. It happens in ordinary churches too. I particularly remember the sense of isolation I felt in one church during the exchange of the Peace. Everyone seemed to know everyone, and they went around kissing and hugging each other. I felt utterly excluded. Often in those situations I make the first move, and people then respond. But on those two particular occasions, when I waited for others to welcome me, I was left alone and felt unwelcome. So I understood Helen from Bristol's feelings when she wrote:

> I am writing on a simple matter but one which I believe is vital to the whole survival of the Church. For a number of years now I have been trying to find a church in which I could settle. The problem which I have encountered repeatedly is simply that no-one will speak. No-one seems prepared to welcome a newcomer in. Frankly, having persevered at a number of churches, I am not surprised that church membership is falling. While I realise there are many complex reasons for this, a welcoming church would go a long way to overcoming some of the difficulties. A welcome pack shoved in an embarrassed way into your hand does not rate high on my list. Could the various churches be approached to see if they have a successful system which might work in other churches? I am sorry to write when there are so many things of importance being discussed in the church today. But perhaps the grass roots remain the most important of all.

Growth at the Grass Roots

The grass roots are indeed crucial to all that this Decade is about. It remains sadly true that far too many congregations in the Church of England remain more interested in maintenance than mission. Many churches do not welcome new members for the simple reason that they do not want new members. A Bob Dylan song contains the words 'he who is not busy being born is busy dying', and thankfully, the Decade of

Evangelism is encouraging increased numbers of parish churches to commit themselves to growth. Alex Wedderspoon, in his book *Grow or Die*, writes:

> The desire for growth arises out of the conviction that if the Christian faith is true then it is true for all, that membership of the Church matters and that those outside the Church are missing something which will enhance their lives. It is a conviction which arises out of a high theology of the Church as the Body of Christ, the living agent of God's saving purpose for individual people and for mankind as a whole.

Church growth is not just about adding extra members to the congregation. New structures may be needed within the Church to meet changing needs and circumstances. Examples of this are the plans in some dioceses for Local Non-Stipendiary Ministry; the fresh emphasis on collaborative ministry between ordained and lay people; and the growing and necessary ministry of ordained women in the Church. As Bishop Lesslie Newbigin has commented:

> The question is not what special and exceptional arrangements must we make in order to keep the traditional pattern of ministry from breaking under the strains? The question is: what in the new circumstances into which God has thrust us is the pattern of ministry which is proper to the nature of the Church as God's apostolic community in the world of today?

Church growth is also to do with the influence of the laity, outside the church building, on the life of the community and the nation. As we have noted, parents, school governors, members of local councils, charity helpers are some obvious examples of this. This kind of growth often comes through the unselfconscious witness of ordinary members of the congregation going about their daily life and work – blossoming where God plants them. All this, of course, depends on spiritual growth – the deepening and renewing of church members in their personal journey of prayer, faith, fellowship and witness that must undergird everything.

Concern For Christian Truth

My sabbatical in the United States studying church growth confirmed for me the 'Grow or Die' thesis that there are certain basic principles which, when applied with faith, vigour and common sense by the Church, make for growth rather than for decline. People respond when faith rather than doubt, and clarity rather than confusion, is communicated in terms they can understand. 'What matters is that clergy and lay leaders have, and are seen to have, a positive and intelligent concern for Christian truth, that they have thought and prayed their way through to certain clear personal beliefs, and are able to communicate their beliefs to ordinary people with conviction and common sense.'

To Fail to Plan is to Plan to Fail

One of the central principles of Church growth is that no Church will ever grow unless it wants to. The Chester Diocese has ten basic questions for every Parochial Church Council to ask itself in developing a strategy for growth.

1. What is your church policy about evangelism? Has it a bias to the excluded? How many others in the church know what the policy is? Do they agree with it? When was its effectiveness last evaluated?
2. In the community in which you are situated what are the main concerns and motivations of the people? Where do they meet? What is the image of the church in the neighbourhood? How much basic Christian knowledge has each age group?
3. How did those in this church become Christians? What

is the proportion of 'cradle' to 'convert' Christians? Did they have a sudden or gradual experience of Christ? How long ago was this? What age were they then? What was the main factor under God which led to their conversion? How far does the policy of the Church build on this data or run counter to it? (It is easiest to sail with the wind of the Spirit.) Are you persisting with inappropriate or out of date methods of evangelism? Is the church locked into only one or two methods?

4. Do the structures of the Church help or hinder evangelism? Is there clutter which needs clearing away? Can existing structures be made more outgoing?

5. Have the evangelists in the church been identified? Are they being: set free, trained, affirmed, encouraged, used?

6. Is the church under the Lordship of Christ so that when he says 'Go' something happens? Are praying people listening for God's guidance?

7. Are the leaders of the church encouraging evangelism – if necessary by speaking the truth in love to the congregation? Or are they so concerned with evangelism that the sheep are not fed and encouraged?

8. How many in the church are really concerned about evangelism? Are they being mobilised and the numbers expanded? Do they understand their faith?

9. Is there a maternity ward permanently available in the church – for enquiries, new Christians, etc.?

10. Motivation is essential. Effective, intelligent evangelism comes from channelled excitement not guilt. Is the full Gospel presented in the power of the Spirit so that the congregation catches fire?

This approach would not appeal to every congregation – but the point is clear. A church which has no plans for growth has plans for no growth. To fail to plan is to plan to fail.

Welcome to Our Church

Growing churches do have certain recognisable features. High on the list – and well in front of all other factors which attract outsiders to join a church is the welcome it offers. Every church, says Wedderspoon, should have a clearly planned ministry of welcome, so that those who come to the church are met in a friendly way by other lay people and put at their ease. This will include providing facilities for young children. Failing to provide crèche facilities for young parents to use if they wish to is tantamount to slamming the church door in their faces. This welcome must include a well-thought out system whereby people coming to church for the first time are recognised and given the opportunity in a sensitive way to become members. It is also important that visitors are able to find out very easily the place and time of church services and activities.

Welcoming the Baptism Party

The first time many people enter a church is for a baptism, wedding or funeral. Some churches now have attractive leaflets specially designed for these occasions. They help people to feel at ease in the church and relate what is happening to them to the Christian faith. The following letter I was sent shows how the right kind of welcome can help:

> My husband and I feel moved to write to you regarding the recent baptism of our son, Stephen. We were not regular churchgoers before the event and we were rather nervous; but we were immediately put at ease. The actual Baptism was really enjoyable and moving. It was a day we will treasure. We now try to attend church regularly and are hoping to start adult confirmation classes soon.
>
> Some friends of ours have never had their children baptised because the local vicar refused as they did not attend church and they refused to attend for a few weeks prior to

the service. It was refreshing to be at a church which works on the principle that gentle persuasion works better than stubborn obstinacy.

Every Sunday a Special Sunday

Imagine you are a visitor to your church next Sunday – uncertain about what you will find there and worried about how you will cope. Will there be a sensitive and warm welcome for you? Will the building look cared for and fresh? Will there be an atmosphere of prayer and worship? Will uplifting worship and lively teaching be matched by a friendly and open fellowship? Will you feel that what is said there speaks to your personal needs? Is there good lay involvement? Do people of every age and condition, from babies in arms to the old and deaf, the single as well as the families, feel cared for? Is it really a church of which you could say after a first visit: 'I felt near to God and the people there made me feel I belonged. I want to go again'?

If the answer is 'yes' then it may be that changes are not necessary. Certainly change for change's sake is never appropriate. But carrying out check lists like this can be valuable, and the answers should be reviewed at regular intervals. There is always room to grow and there are always key points to watch out for. I picked up from my research in the United States the importance of planning for every Sunday to be a 'special' Sunday.

Lively teaching means a clear and positive sermon, spoken from the heart, well illustrated from everyday life and the Bible. It means group study of the Bible, the meaning of faith, how to pray, and how to live a Christian life. It also means an imaginative programme of teaching for children – to coincide with the main service, since a key factor in drawing young married adults to church is a well-organised Sunday School or Junior Church. It not only nurtures the young, but acts as a highly effective means of reaching out to unchurched families.

Giving Back to God

A growing church is never a one-man band. It is a church where everyone's gifts are recognised and drawn out. Its leaders have the ability to inspire, motivate and teach. It is a church of the laity, in which one of the chief functions of the ordained is to motivate and release every member for mission. Every Christian is called to offer back in service the gifts God has given, which includes money.

Christian discipleship is about offering ourselves completely to God for twenty-four hours a day, seven days a week. A Christian cannot say of anything: 'This is my business and not God's'. In some churches, the moment that point is related to money a barrier goes up: 'Sorry, but that is my private affair.' Of course, that barrier is not about money: it is about faith. All too often, church members think of giving for God's church as if it were a financial issue, but at heart it is not, it is a spiritual one. In churches where that is taught and understood, the barrier goes down and an enormous amount of generosity is released.

A change of attitude towards giving is necessary in many congregations. The story of Christianity shows that when people are courageous and take risks in their giving, they are richly blessed. When giving stands still – which in real financial terms means reduces – then vision soon goes and the life and mission of that church starts to wither away.

Fishers and Shepherds

Jesus told Peter he would make him a fisher of men (Mark 1:17). He told that same disciple 'Feed my sheep' (John 20:17). In Christian mission shepherding and fishing go together. That is why evangelism which is separated from pastoral care is likely to be manipulative.

One of the arts of fishing is learning how to be patient: too much noise and activity will frighten the fish away. It would be wise not to forget that in this Decade of Evangelism. The Anglican way is well described in words from the Archbishop of Canterbury:

> From my experience, effective evangelism has often flowed out of the life and ministry of a church living the faith: the faithful visiting and speaking of the love of God; the regular preaching of God's word; the faithful administration of the sacraments of the Church; the joyful worship and fellowship of the local body of Christ. Hardly exciting stuff most of the time, but the way most churches grow.

6

Confronting

Facing Failure

A vicar and a group from his church council came to see me
bewildered and distressed. They had prayed and planned. They
had tried to bring about, in a sensitive and courageous way,
some of the changes they felt their worship and ministry and
church structures needed. But the result of all their efforts had
been the loss of some members. There had been no numerical
gain.

We must not fall into the trap of thinking that the Decade
of Evangelism is only about attendance ratings and worldly
success. That would be a travesty of the Gospel. We live in a
culture which rates success highly. The media looks for instant
results – mocks when there are none. If, after we have prayer-
fully done our best to pass on the good news of Jesus, nothing
positive seems to have happened, we must not lose heart. We
follow a master who was despised and rejected; whose ministry
ended in being beaten and nailed on a cross; and whose followers mostly deserted him at the end. Even Easter Day began
in tears. During this Decade some churches will watch others
seem to succeed where they seem to fail – and, like the group
that visited me, they will feel rejected, beaten and tearful.
It may help us to remember Paul's words to the Corinthian
Church:

> We are often troubled, but not crushed; sometimes in doubt
> but never in despair; there are many enemies, but we are
> never without a friend; and though badly hurt at times, we

are never destroyed . . . We know that God, who raised the
Lord Jesus to life, will also raise us up with Jesus and take
us, together with you, into his presence . . . For this reason
we never become discouraged.

Tears For the World

It is no accident that there is a cross on the cover of this book.
The Gospel we proclaim is about Christ crucified and risen. It
is a message of joy and hope; but it could not be so without
the wounds of love. Perhaps the most poignant and certainly
most disturbing picture is the tearful black face looking at an
empty plate. If our Gospel is not about confronting that pain
and injustice, then it is not worth proclaiming.

On a recent pilgrimage to the Holy Land we visited the
church of Dominus Flevit. It is halfway down the Mount of
Olives on the traditional site where Jesus wept over the city of
Jerusalem (Luke 19:41–4). We used there a lovely meditation
from H J Richards' guide, *Pilgrim to the Holy Land*:

Lord Jesus Christ,
    today we share your tears for the cities of the world;
    – still we have not loved the things that make for peace.

We weep for the divided cities:
    where brother fights with brother,
where anger feeds on hatred,
where prejudice blinds the eyes of compassion,
and even religion divides,
where children are taught to hate,
    and old men relish ancient wrongs.

We weep for the cities of oppression:
    where iron law imprisons freedom,
where thought is curbed and conscience stifled,
where the questioning spirit is called a traitor,

where art and civilising truth grow barren,
    and each must think in manner as his neighbour.

We weep for the cities of poverty:
    where children live, but die too soon,
where eager hands can find no work,
where hunger rules and aid is short,
where mothers clutch uncomprehending young,
    and where the little we could do, we fail to do.

We weep for our cities, and for ourselves;
    We have not learned the things that make for peace.

Lord,
    turn tears to love,
and love to work.
Turn work to justice,
    and all that makes for peace.

Jesus' Manifesto

These words echo the quotation from Isaiah 61:1–2 which Jesus used at the very start of his ministry: 'The Spirit of the Lord is upon me, because he has chosen me to bring good news to the poor. He has sent me to proclaim liberty to the captives and recovery of sight to the blind; to set free the oppressed and announce the time has come when the Lord will save his people.'

Luke chapter 4 shows that when Jesus went on to spell out what that meant, and to speak as if gentiles were specially favoured by God, the people in the synagogue tried to kill him. This was not the kind of good news they wanted to hear. The same may turn out to be true in this Decade. What Jesus called the good news may be unpalatable to some, which is why evangelism should never be equated with church growth. A church which is courageous enough to spread the good news of Jesus Christ might even lose some of its members.

Treasuring the Unattractive

The treasuring of the unattractive was a message to which Jesus returned later in his ministry: 'When Lord, did we ever see you hungry and feed you; or thirsty and give you drink. When did we ever see you a stranger and welcome you in our homes – or naked and clothe you? When did we ever see you sick, or in prison, and visit you?' And the answer? 'I tell you, whenever you did this for one of the least important of these brothers of mine, you did it for me.'

What Decade of Evangelism can ignore the words of Jesus telling us to see him in those whom we may feel inclined to steer clear of – the inadequates, the misfits – who perhaps repel us rather than attract us. That is why this Decade must not be allowed to degenerate into strident marches and tub-thumping messages. It is not, as all too many evangelists claim, about bringing Christ to others. It is about seeing the Christ who is already there, and helping others to find him there.

Evangelism or Evangelisation?

There have been fears that a call to evangelism may so empha-sise the call to personal salvation that issues of injustice and need are ignored. But, as a statement from the Anglican Mis-sion Agencies makes clear: 'We cannot confess "Jesus is Lord" without serious consequences for the ordering of the political and economic relationships of humankind and the harmony in which we live as part of the whole creation.'

The Roman Catholic Church has explained its preference for using the word 'evangelisation' rather than 'evangelism'. It says that spreading the good news is a task with many facets. Part of that task is to support and develop the situations in society which conform to the Gospel; another part is to challenge and confront those which do not. A paper for the English Catholic Bishops Conference puts it like this:

This intimate connection between conversion, community and society is at the heart of Catholic belief about the Christian way. This is precisely the reason why we define evangelisation in terms which cover the whole range of activities from proclamation of Christ, to hearing the word, personal conversion to him, membership of his community, and action to bring his teaching alive in the world. We also emphasise the necessary connection between the elements in the process. An emphasis on the necessity of the connection between the elements in the process is characteristic of evangelisation. Evangelism tends to stop with highlighting the first two or three.

Social Action and Evangelism

The Church of England's Steering Group has made it clear that evangelism should, like evangelisation, highlight all those elements, including personal commitment to Christ and social action for peace and justice. It would be a pity if too much time were spent on drawing distinctions between the two words. It is the problem of abstract nouns again, which would have been avoided if we had decided on a Decade of Evangelising! The wholeness of meaning is developed in a scholarly way by Professor Walter Wink of New York Theological Seminary in his major work *Principalities and Powers*:

> Evangelism is always a form of social action . . . The repugnance with which most liberal Christians regard evangelism betrays their own failure to discern that all liberation involves conversion. Whenever evangelism is carried out in full awareness of the Powers, whether in confronting those in power or liberating those crushed by it, proclaiming the sovereignty of Christ is, by that very act, a critique of injustice and idolatry.

The converse, he says, is equally true.

Social action is always evangelism if carried out in full awareness of Christ's sovereignty over the Powers . . . Too often
our social action has been as devoid of spirituality as our
evangelism has been politically innocuous. Too often we
have told the Powers that they were wrong but not whose
they are.

The Church is Only a Sign of the Kingdom

The important thing for local churches is to be aware of the
close link in evangelism between personal commitment and
social action. Some Christians will always find it difficult to
resist the temptation to escape from the realities of the world
into the private sanctuary of a personal love affair with Jesus.
The Decade of Evangelism is a call for discipleship to be lived
out in the world, not in the cosy cocoon of the comfortable
church. The baptismal call is to fight against sin, the world and
the devil, and that means battling against sinful social structures, and devilish political policies and economic exploitation.
As Dag Hammarskjold put it: 'In our age, the road to holiness
necessarily passes through the world of action.'

Writing in the Southwell and Oxford Papers on Contemporary Society, Eric Forshaw ended his critical reflections on the
Decade thus:

My best hope for the Church of England in the Decade is
that a long, deep and compassionate exposure to the rest of
the world beyond its narrow sectional interests, might lead
to a lasting transformation of the now dominant ethos. There
can be no sense in which it can become a sign of the rule of
God whilst it languishes in its present condition. The Church
is only ever the sign of the Kingdom of God, never the
Kingdom itself. If the Decade succeeds in turning the Church
out into the world, to follow God where the Spirit is leading,
then not only will it have received new life in Christ but

become itself the agent of change for the sake of God's Kingdom.

Paul's Damascus Road Conversion

One of the most dramatic stories of change in the New Testament is the story of Paul's conversion on the Damascus Road (Acts 9). It is likely to be used often in this decade as a model, so it is helpful to understand what really happened. It was not a conversion from a secular way of life to following the way of God, which is how it is sometimes presented. Saul was already a devout Jew. The point was that Saul came to realise God was not to be found just in the pious devotions of personal faith. The blinding truth which came upon him was that God was to be found among the oppressed – the very ones he, Saul, was persecuting. The face of the persecuted was the face of Jesus. That is what Paul's conversion was about – seeing Jesus in the oppressed and persecuted and realising his own part in that. In the same way, a conversion experience for people in this generation may be to see, for the first time, the face of Jesus in the human devastation of war or an earthquake. To see the face of Jesus in the tearful, starving faces of Africa – and realise our part, often of unrealised collusion, in the famine, oppression, persecution and killing.

Far too many of the special projects and activities for this Decade are churchy ones. They are unlikely to lead anyone to a truly Pauline kind of conversion. Instead, churchy approaches to evangelism may do the opposite, and lead us backwards to the point where Saul was before the Damascus Road. That was when he was in the business of strident trumpeting, getting his worship right and working on his own personal life of devotion to God.

It cannot be said too often that the call to individual holiness must not, and cannot, be separated from the call to justice in the world. As Dr Charles Elliott, former Director of Christian Aid, has said: 'If we are to take global injustice seriously, we have to start by dealing with the roots of that injustice in each one of us. To fail to do that with ultimate seriousness is to flirt with the role of the hypocrite.'

Confronting Injustice

How do we confront injustice with the redeeming love of Christ? If we do it in a spirit of anger and condemnation then that will show how little progress we have made on our own inward journey. In his book, *Comfortable Compassion?*, Charles Elliott suggests we confront injustice in a way which achieves the following objectives:

1. Reveals the effects of injustice on the poor and vulnerable.
2. Places us alongside those who suffer those effects. In other words, it has to be a real confrontation and not simply a cosy chat between those in collusion.
3. Raises questions about the system, the structure, the Powers themselves, rather than about its agents.
4. Looks for total transformation, not ameliorative reform.
5. Accepts that the consequences of such a challenge will often be unpleasant. In some countries that can mean death, even at the hands of the religious establishment.
6. Accepts that the process of confrontation does not, of itself, transform structures. It may challenge them, educate them, shock them into deeper awareness of what their essence looks like from the bottom. In the end, however, transformation is the work of the Spirit.
7. Sees, therefore, the process of structural transformation as a gift we all need to share.

All this takes time, effort, imagination, discipline, perseverance and pain. 'As we confront the powers that dominate us and our structures, and as we explore how we are incorporated into the cosmic drama, both in its conflict and, 'in Christ', its final outcome, we are likely to discover that we share in the wounds of the universe – and we contribute our wounds to the universe. It is in that discovery of our woundedness that we both share in, and are healed by, the Cross of Christ, and are thereby gradually freed from the grip of the Powers that dominate us.'

Speak Out

The Lambeth Conference of 1988 defended firmly the right and duty of Christians to speak out and act on social issues. The bishops saw this duty as flowing directly from the belief that this is God's world. For Christians not to attempt to confront such matters would imply that the religious dimension is irrelevant, which would be a surrender to secularism. There are many stories of oppression and injustice across the world. Racism, torture, starvation, death are all familiar to us from our television screens; the forces of evil are everywhere and growing. The tragedy is that many people of goodwill remain silent or align themselves with those who have the power to change things but do not. The Conference report said:

> The need to speak and to act is urgent. Christians are called to be faithful to Christ and to the Word of God where he always and unconditionally stands alongside the poor, the disadvantaged and the oppressed. The people of God ought, therefore, to be the voice of those whose voice has been silenced and suppressed, speaking and acting not necessarily on a political party platform but out of Christian conviction about the God who demands justice and whose will is peace and reconciliation.

Positive Discrimination to the Poor

At the start of this Decade of Evangelism more than 800 million people are trapped in absolute poverty – a condition of life so

characterised by malnutrition, illiteracy, disease, squalid sur-
roundings, high infant mortality and low life expectancy as to
be beneath any reasonable definition of human decency. The
world's largest deprived and needy group is that of mothers who
have sole responsibility for dependent children. In Calcutta a
quarter of a million people of all ages are homeless. Even in
London 10,000 people sleep out in the streets. The material
poverty of the destitute and powerless is a social evil which
degrades and stunts the image of God in us all. When Jesus
said, quoting Deuteronomy 15:11, 'The poor you will always
have with you' (Mark 14:7), he was not encouraging com-
placency or indifference but persistence in the battle to over-
come poverty. The cruel and devastating contrast between
affluence and poverty within and between nations is a scandal.
Behind every cup of coffee and every slice of lemon in a drink
there is a story of what to every Christian ought to be absolutely
unacceptable poverty and exploitation.

The theologian Gustavo Gutierrez has spoken of the difficulty of proclaiming the Gospel in this situation. It is not like
the problem which Bonhoeffer faced in the 1930s and 1940s –
of how to talk of God to a person 'come of age' in the twentieth
century; 'It is how to proclaim the living God in a situation of
death'. The poor die before their time. In Zambia the average
life span in some areas is forty-one years. In Europe it is around
seventy-five.

At the Lambeth Conference in 1988, Gutierrez said:

In view of the present situation there have been many advo-
cates of a preference for and solidarity with the poor. There
is no favouritism here, no glorification of the poor as if they
were innocent of sin, but a genuine recognition that they
have been sinned against, which justifies the need for positive
discrimination in witness to the inauguration of the Kingdom.
Poverty in my life is my material problem. Poverty in the
lives of 800 million human beings is my moral and spiritual
problem. Affluence should not be allowed to stifle our con-

science or sap our wills in the work for the eradication of poverty.

Urban Priority Areas

In England, the *Faith in the City* report of 1988 was a comprehensive analysis of the social, economic and spiritual problems which confront people who live in the old industrial inner cities and on post-war housing estates. Its basic message is as valid as it ever was. Those who live there are important to God, to the Church and to the nation. A great deal of work still needs to be done to raise awareness of issues such as employment, housing and education, and to tackle them in the light of Gospel principles.

The follow-up report *Living Faith in the City*, published in 1990, devotes a section to evangelism and urban priority areas. On a typical Sunday less than 1% of the adult population of a UPA will be worshipping in the parish church.

> This must not lead us into the error of supposing that urban parishioners are accordingly more godless or 'secular' than those in the suburbs or rural localities. Undeniably UPAs present particular difficulties, so that (for example) even the vicar may find it impossible to negotiate the security system protecting a block of flats in his parish. Yet the evangelistic task is urgent, and unless the company of committed disciples is increased there will often not be enough of them to participate fully in the various opportunities for service within their local communities.
>
> Time and again it has been proved that when a congregation in a tough situation becomes aware of its vulnerability, and the irrelevance of many of the traditional structures of church life, significant and sometimes exciting developments occur. Christians in such places are driven to their knees in humble submission to the will of God and a readiness to bear the cross through costly involvement in their local com-

munity. Where there is interaction between theological tradition, the Bible, and engagement with issues thrown up by
the world's agenda, a spirituality is forged which is often
unknown in other parts of the Church.

All this says much about the centrality of hope in the Christian
journey – as bright vision is tested by dark reality. The report
quotes Matthew Arnold writing about a minister in a notorious
Victorian UPA who kept going by focusing his ministry on
Christ:

> Was August and the fierce sun overhead
> Smote on the squalid slums of Bathing Green,
> And the pale weaver, through his window seen
> In Spitalfields, looked thrice dispirited
>
> I met a preacher there I knew, and said:
> 'Ill and reworked, how fare you in this scene?'
> 'Bravely', said he, 'for I of late have been
> Much cheered with thoughts of Christ, the living bread.'

Spirituality Which has Ceased to Struggle

Living Faith in the City emphasised the importance of prayer
and spirituality. Thankfully, it is a common theme in almost
all the literature for this decade – and rightly so. But it must
be true to the Gospel we are called to proclaim. Kenneth
Leech, who has sharply criticised the Decade of Evangelism,
has sounded a warning about current spirituality. He argues
that within the assumptions of our present culture, rather than
in conflict with it, there is a particular kind of so-called spirituality which is being promoted as if it were just another product
on the market. His complaint is that the proponents of this
spiritual industry offer methods of meditation and all kinds of
techniques and self-understanding, but they operate within and
do not question the existing unjust order. 'Such spirituality
lacks the imaginative encounter with the reality of poverty, pain

and dereliction. Yet spirituality which has ceased to struggle, to hurt, to disturb and challenge, is no longer Christian.' Without that commitment to confront, to care for those in need and seek justice for the oppressed, it is not possible to speak of orthodox Christianity. In an article in *The Independent* Kenneth Leech wrote:

> A major problem . . . is that much contemporary spirituality is not biblically rooted – hence its lack of concern for the poor and the demands of justice, and its lack of recognition that spiritual life includes prophetic rage against those who oppress the poor through unjust laws and neglect . . . A spirituality able to provide resources for the struggle against poverty must be one which is concerned with truth, with equality, and with vision – all of which involve alternative ways of thinking and imagining reality. Like all spiritual discipline, it begins with the unmasking of illusion, of false consciousness, of that refusal to face reality which is so endemic to the maintenance of injustice.

7

Proclaiming

A Gospel to Proclaim

At every ordination ceremony in the Church of England the
deacon or priest being ordained is asked: 'Will you, then, in
the strength of the Holy Spirit, continually stir up the gift that
is in you, to make Christ known to all?' Immediately after that
comes the prayer: 'Enlighten your ministers with knowledge
and understanding, that by their teaching and their lives they
may proclaim your word.' The bishop specifically tells the
priests 'to proclaim the word of the Lord' in the declaration
and, later, in the blessing asks that God may give grace and
power to them 'to proclaim the gospel of your salvation'. In
the proper preface for communion at the ordination we give
thanks to God because 'you ordain ministers to proclaim the
word'. The call to proclaim features regularly in Anglican
worship – not least in its hymns. Most congregations are familiar with the hymn *We Have a Gospel to Proclaim*. In short,
there can be no doubt that the Church of England has a clear
commitment to proclaim the Gospel.

What Is the Gospel?

William Abraham in his important book *The Logic of Evangelism* puts forward a definition of the Gospel, beginning by saying
what it is not. The Gospel, he says, is not a set of arguments
about divine order. It is not the expression of religious experience brought to verbal form. It is not about a romantic aware-

ness of God in nature. It is not a philosophical theory about the nature of ultimate reality. It is not a set of moral maxims to improve the world. It is not a legalistic lament about human nature. It is not a sentimental journey into ancient history.

> It is the unique narrative of what God has done to inaugurate his kingdom in Jesus of Nazareth, crucified outside Jerusalem, risen from the dead, seated at the right hand of God, and now reigning eternally with the Father, through the activity of the Holy Spirit, in the Church and in the world.

As Paul makes clear in Romans 10:13–15, if that Gospel is not announced, it will not be known. Quoting Joel's prophecy that everyone who calls out to the Lord for help will be saved, Paul asks how people can call for that help if they have not believed: 'And how can they believe if they have not heard the message? And how can they hear if the message is not proclaimed? And how can the message be proclaimed if messengers are not sent out?'

Proclaim in Order to Initiate

Dr Abraham goes on to say the good news of the kingdom should be transmitted with flair and in culturally fitting forms. It should be heralded less in the church and more in the marketplace. Furthermore, the announcing or gossiping of the Gospel should include the invitation to respond in faith and repentance. The whole process must be soaked in prayer and sensitivity to the Holy Spirit.

> Both the word proclaimed and the invitation to respond are staggering in their proportions and utterly incredible to most people who stop to think about them. They need, therefore, not just the witness of the speaker as expressed in his or her sincerity and integrity, for that would be a weak reed to rely on; they need also the inward, mysterious, numinous witness

of the Holy Spirit who alone can convict the world of sin, of righteousness and judgement.

Much that poses for evangelism fosters prejudice and encourages pride. Often there are emotional calls for the nation once again to be Christian. Ultimately, Abraham claims, this kind of plea is corrupting.

It makes the gospel of the kingdom a means to an end. It cuts proclamation loose from Christian initiation. It makes Christianity an adjunct to a nationalistic ideology that undercuts the transcendence of the kingdom. It impedes the transformation of culture and politics that the coming of the kingdom should inspire. The only real antidote to this is to insist that proclamation be carried out with the express intention to initiate people into the reign of God. Every other intention should be set aside as sub-Christian and inadequate.

Evangelicals, Catholics and the Mainstream

The reluctance of the Church of England Steering Group to include 'proclaiming' in its mission statement reflects some of those concerns, which are widely shared throughout the Church of England. Whilst it is true that recent debates in the General Synod have emphasised the evangelical and catholic sides of churchmanship, most churches still belong to the mainstream middle. They are neither particularly catholic nor particularly evangelical. That is the heartland of Anglicanism and it is the part which remains the most hesitant about the Decade of Evangelism.

When the Decade was launched, I asked that each local church should engage in evangelism 'in ways authentic to their own tradition'. Not surprisingly, the evangelicals were quickly to the fore in their distinctive enthusiasm for spreading the Gospel. The catholic wing, which, though committed in principle is sometimes more defensive has also produced some excellent material for the decade. The Archbishops' *Spring-*

board initiative will further heighten the profile of the evangelical and catholic wings, though both Bishop Michael Marshall and Canon Michael Green have gone out of their way to offer their services to the whole Church. Nevertheless, it is a pity that *Springboard* could not have included a third leader from within the mainstream middle of the Anglican tradition who could have related in an unthreatening but challenging way to the majority of people who belong to, or look to, the Church of England. Most Anglicans in this country shy away from either the catholic or evangelical label, and most still equate evangelism with the evangelicals.

The Anglican Style

The breakthrough for the Church of England in this decade will be the owning of an authentic style of Anglican evangelism by the mainstream. It will be characterised by the kind of guidelines for passing on the good news which have been suggested by the modern spiritual writer Henri Nouwen in his book, *Reaching Out*:

> Remain convinced without being rigid
> Willing to confront without being officious
> Gentle and forgiving without being soft
> A true witness without being manipulative
> Conveying above all else in our very presence
> The love that is Christ.

Come Gracious Spirit, Heavenly Dove

It is becoming increasingly fashionable in 'decade circles' to talk about the Holy Spirit only in terms of power and fire. There are many ways in which the Holy Spirit is referred to in the Bible – such as the creating spirit and the oil that gladdens and consecrates people's hearts. Nevertheless, on the Day of

Pentecost there was a powerful noise which sounded like wind
and it did seem as if tongues of fire touched each person.
During his ministry Jesus himself said: 'I came to set the earth
on fire, and how I wish it were already kindled' (Luke 12:49).
So it is understandable that phrases like 'fanning the flame' are
popular, and Brunner's famous axiom that 'as fire exists for
burning' so also 'the Church exists for mission' is much quoted.

The danger is that this kind of language can seem aggressive.
As we know to our cost in this country, communities and
individuals are inflamed all too easily by anger and, literally,
set on fire. Unthinking use of such words is likely to be insensitive and counterproductive for passing on the good news of
Jesus.

Another word now much in use is 'power': as the modern
hymn puts it, 'We are building a people of power'. Evangelism
has often had about it a rogue tendency towards triumphalism
and success which is far removed from the good news of a man
who, before he rose from the dead, became powerless and was
nailed to a cross. As Michael Ramsey warned those who separate the experience of the Holy Spirit from the historical events
of the Gospel: 'It is a costly thing to invoke the Spirit, for the
glory of Calvary was the cost of the Spirit's mission and is the
cost of the Spirit's renewal. It is in the shadow of the cross that
in any age of history Christians pray: Come, Holy Spirit.'

The more appropriate symbol for the Holy Spirit in this
Decade of Evangelism is the dove. At Jesus' baptism, while he
was praying, 'the Holy Spirit came down upon him in bodily
form like a dove. And a voice came from heaven, "You are
my own dear Son. I am pleased with you" ' (Luke 3:21-2).
The sign of the dove is, therefore, a reminder of baptism. A
chief aim of this Decade is to inspire every baptised member
of the Church to be one of its forefront missionaries.

From the story of the dove with the olive branch in its beak
at the time of the Flood (Genesis 8:11), the dove has been a
sign of being gentle and forgiving, of peace and reconciliation.
'Peace I leave with you; my peace I give to you; not as the
world gives do I give to you' (John 14:27).

Speaking of the graciousness of the Holy Spirit at work in Northern Ireland, Archbishop Robin Eames said: 'I have seen example after example of attitudes of forgiveness, people reaching out to each other over the obstacles, lives formerly devoted to acts of hatred or revenge transformed into living witness to the love of Christ.' That is evangelism. Few who heard him will forget Gordon Wilson, the man whose daughter was killed beside him in the Remembrance Day bombing at Enniskillen. That night he spoke on television about his personal loss and devastation. His forgiveness and lack of bitterness spoke volumes to millions. It was a proclaiming of the Gospel of love and peace.

Coping With Our Differences

One of the joys in this Decade is church music. There is a rich tradition of music within the Church of England, owing much to the evangelical and catholic revivals of the last century, and times of renewal within the Church almost always give birth to new music. Harry Bramma, Director of the Royal School of Church Music, hopes to see in this decade spiritual enrichment and renewal of the worship in all our churches through the God-given power of music. As he says, music has the power to touch the hearts and minds of men and women in a remarkable way. It has healing power, bringing assurance in every kind of grief. Nothing helps to unite people in bonds of fellowship more than music. It also helps us to look upwards. In the Quarterly Magazine of the Royal School of Church Music, Harry Bramma wrote:

An act of worship should always make people aware of the immense majesty and transcendence of God. Music, above all other means of human expression, has the power to make 'the house of God' into 'the gate of heaven'. So often worship is earthbound. We must do all we can to give it wings and to restore, through skilful use of music, much of what has been lost in our chattering liturgies.

Unfortunately, music can all too often be the cause of a collapse of relationships within a church. A polarising of those who prefer the traditional style and those who like the modern leads to an inevitable clash. Yet even here there is an evangelistic opportunity. The way we cope with our differences can sometimes be the very thing that attracts others to our faith.

One of the great strengths of the Church of England has been its ability to steer a middle course between two extremes, and that can be achieved very successfully with church music. I have been to some very inspiring acts of worship in which the traditional choir and organ and the instrumental group and singers brought together the best of the old and the new. On a national level, the ecumenical and generally traditional Royal School of Church Music is now linked to the Music in Worship Foundation which encourages renewal music.

The Gospel Must Not Be Trivialised

Many of the new hymns and music will not last. That has always been true: only 0.4% of Charles Wesley's hymns are still sung today. But it has to be said that there is little to compare between Wesley's words and the lyrics of many modern spiritual songs. Mainstream Anglicans do not take easily to what is sometimes referred to as 'happy clappy' worship, and although this is partly cultural, it is also because many of the lyrics are too trite. We need to be wary of approaches to evangelism which see the Christian faith in terms of a simplistic and neatly packaged theology which will provide an easy answer to every question. The Roman Catholic journal, *The Tablet*, warned at the start of the Decade of Evangelism:

Simplistic doctrine and simplistic moral teaching are bound to boomerang, for in the long run they cannot satisfy the profound instinct for truth . . . The Church is, and must be seen to offer, what is greater than, and beyond, the natural reach of ourselves and our human capacities if it is to attract respect and attention. If the Christian evangelist reduces the vast mystery of faith to a few lines that might come off a corn-flake packet, or offers slick moral answers as if they can be drawn out of a machine, he is dealing in cartoons, not masterpieces, and sowing cynicism and derision rather than faith . . .

The temptation to reduce Christian truths to Christmas cracker phrases is often well intentioned, but we should not be surprised if it ends in provoking uneasiness and contempt. The temptation to offer processed food, slick answers, easy sentimentalities, slogans and jingles, as representing the mind and heart of Almighty God and the awesome mysteries of salvation, may be powerful in an increasingly shallow culture, but there comes a point when even the laziest consumers begin to realise it damages the health . . . Better for people to shrink from the Gospel because it is too great than because it is too small.

The Gospel is never about giving easy answers to life's deepest needs and problems. One of the most memorable pictures of the Crucifixion that I have ever seen showed the body of Jesus hanging in a shape which looked rather like a question mark. The point is that the Gospel challenge asks questions of us. Life with Jesus is not easy. It is full of questions, and it is about carrying a cross. The good news is not that all problems are solved, but that we are given the strength to keep going, knowing that nothing that lies ahead of us is greater than God's love behind us.

Healing is Part of Proclaiming

One of the significant features of recent church life has been the rediscovery of the ministry of healing. It is a collaborative ministry in which both clergy and laity can be involved. In the

New Testament, healing and evangelism invariably go together. Jesus did not intend the good news to be proclaimed by word alone, and the healing of the sick in the name of Jesus is as much part of the proclamation of the kingdom as the passing on of the good news.

On some occasions, the Decade of Evangelism has unwittingly become an umbrella for healing ministries which take little note of the pain of Gethsemane or the message of the Cross. In his Henry Cooper Memorial lecture on Healing and Evangelism, Trevor Nash said that if the healing ministry is to have any credibility, then proper consideration must be given to the fact of pain and continuing anguish. They must not be ignored or belittled. 'We need to keep faith with those who bear in their bodies, and minds and emotions, the marks of the crucified and risen Lord, while they grow in wholeness from day to day.'

The ministry of healing, like the ministry of evangelising, is not about the healthy visiting the sick. In our different ways, we are all sick. 'As we recognise our mutual sickness, the Christ in each of us is able to minister to both of us. Have you noticed how often you leave a sick room restored and more aware of our risen Lord than when you entered?' In healing, as in evangelism, the Cross is central to any realistic and credible preaching of Christ's healing work. People can be easily misled by descriptions of a glossy resurrection with no Cross, and the result can often be that their deepest needs have not been met. What is important is that at each laying on of hands we are being made one with Christ. There is no other healer but him.

The Importance of Touch

There are times when words fail to express what we want to say. At such moments the gentle squeeze of a hand or an arm round a shoulder can speak volumes. It can be a means of expressing what is always the ultimately inexpressible love of

God. Touch plays an important part in healing – and not just in the laying on of hands. Trevor Nash explains:

> The significance of touch in human life cannot be over-stressed. When we are comforting those in distress we may used the gift of touch. It has to be done very sensitively. When we exchange the Peace in the Eucharist, let us be very sensitive towards the person with whom we are exchanging it. Sometimes it can be insensitive and it is not surprising that the stranger who is caught up in it perhaps does not come the next Sunday because they are hurt. It is too much. They are overwhelmed. Other parishes, of course, seem rather more a collection of cold fish and in a few others it doesn't happen at all. All I am really saying is let us be very sensitive in the giving of the Peace and remember that sometimes the person who is the stranger beside us may not have been touched for thirty or forty years.

I have little doubt that sensitivity and thoughtfulness are among the greatest evangelistic gifts. When in our language we say that we are touched by something, it does not necessarily mean a physical touch. More often it refers to a little act of kindness which showed that someone had listened, and noticed and cared. That is the love of God in action and nearer to the proclaiming of the Gospel than many a spoken word.

The New Age Movement

We live in a materialistic culture in which spirituality is frequently described in wholly human and materialistic terms. A very important feature of the Decade of Evangelism is the current examination of the relationship between the Gospel and contemporary culture. One feature being studied is the challenge of the New Age movement. The term New Age is an umbrella for a whole host of ideas – many of them to do with the occult. Its followers look to the dawn of the new astrological Age of Aquarius. This they believe will be a time when all the disasters that have plagued this century will be transformed by a new understanding of the natural world. Denuded forests, holes in the ozone layer, pollution, famine and war will be no more. New Agers also believe in a spirituality unshackled by dogma, whose mystical power will transform their lives and bring them new purpose.

Disturbingly, a growing number of people look to the movement to fill the spiritual void within them. Lawrence Osborn, a conference organiser for 'The Gospel and Our Culture' points out that their very existence is an indictment of Christianity, for New Agers are the very people for whom Christianity should have proved attractive. In an article in the *Church of England Newspaper* he states that two-thirds of all New Agers have tried the Church and found it wanting.

> They see Christians who are uncomfortable about the supernatural aspects of Christian faith and belief, and Christian institutions which reflect the unacceptable face of secular institutions through personality cults, dishonesty, corruption, the disempowerment of the laity, racism and sexism.

Some serious attempts are now being made to build bridges of understanding between the thinking and spirituality of the New Age movement and Christianity. The Omega Order near Bristol is one example of this attempt, although it is not without its critics within the Church. Michael Perry's new book *Gods Within* is a recent and useful critique of the movement from a Christian viewpoint. Lawrence Osborn points out that concerns such as the environment, wholeness and a relational view of reality can all be found in orthodox Christian theology. That so many Christians are suspicious of them is a measure of the extent to which Christianity has been subverted by Enlightenment thought.

> Only when we have demonstrated by word and deed that we understand and sympathise with their concerns will we be in a position to share the Good News . . . The Challenge is to

understand and love the New Agers. Only then will we have the right to confront them with the gospel.

Decade for Repair of the Earth

The 1990s have been designated by the United Nations as a 'decade for the repair of the earth'. Noting this, the same Lambeth Conference which called for the Decade of Evangelism also urged Christians to recognise that concern for the environment is concern for God's world. The world is a gift to us from God. It is to be revered and cared for as his, not ours. Together with all people of good will, Christians must learn again to cherish the God-given resources of the earth, through responsible stewardship of technology and of the environment.

In one of the most powerful reports to emerge from the Lambeth Conference, there is a clear warning:

> . . . as the Church proclaims that God is reconciling the world to himself, so it has a responsibility to see that people do not become alienated from the life of God and his world by the misuse of technology and the destruction of the environment . . . The fight against pollution, erosion, waste, and all devastation of natural territories and human communities, is a necessary and direct expression of their faith in God. It is a part of the Church's prophetic role to proclaim that faith cannot be disembodied and Christians may not behave as if such evils did not exist in the world.

The use of the word 'proclaim' in this section is no accident. Certainly a Church committed to proclaiming the Gospel cannot ignore the ecological issues which face us in this Decade. The contrast between the environment today and in the time of Jesus is vividly expressed by Michael Crosby in his *Spirituality of the Beatitudes*:

> In Jesus' day part of life's unity came from the birds in the sky (Matthew 6:26). Today oil slicks wash them ashore, and

we are broken. Wild flowers and grass in the field (Matthew 6:28, 30) brought spontaneous joy. Today the fact that chemicals leave the land barren makes us weep. Jesus spoke in parables about picking grapes from thorn-bushes, figs from prickly plants, and good fruit from decayed trees (Matthew 7:16–18). Today cash crops from the poor nations support the lifestyle of rich nations like ours and create for us a harvest of shame.

Shaking Hands With Other Denominations

A key test for the Churches in this Decade will be the way in which, despite all the disappointments there have been over unity and the cooling down of enthusiasm for it, trust is developed between the denominations through shared evangelism. There is much that divides – issues of authority and ministry, birth control and divorce – but if we uphold that oft-quoted ecumenical dictum, that we should do together all that we are not in conscience obliged to do separately, then we can undoubtedly make Christ known together.

A problem arises when we move on to initiate new Christians into the Kingdom. To which denomination will they be drawn? These are matters which have yet to be explored in depth by the newly appointed Churches Group for Evangelisation, which meets under the umbrella of Churches Together in England. The Decade began with much interdenominational co-operation and enthusiasm. There has been some cooling off whilst the different Churches worked out the particular styles they wish to adopt, but for the sake of the Gospel the Churches Together must be seen to be together in proclaiming the good news.

Half-believers

Within the Churches the hand of friendship must counter what the Archbishop of York has described as an ugly possessiveness creeping into Christianity. 'I detect a certain meanness creeping in to some forms of the Christian faith, attempts to ration God's grace, to lay down rules for receiving it, to exclude and dismiss the wistful half-believers who sense something important and magical about Christmas, but cannot put it into orthodox words. I am not saying orthodox words don't matter, but we don't begin there. We begin with God's generosity towards those who don't deserve it.'

There is a tendency among those who are most enthusiastic about evangelising to categorise people who attend church as either being 'real' Christians or not. It is this kind of attitude which puts off the mainstream Anglicans. We are all at different stages on our spiritual journey: only God knows the point each of us has reached. The one thing of which we can be certain is that he loves us, and everyone ought to be able to find that love reflected in his Church. Creating a loving atmosphere for the stranger and the half-believer is more important than working out great plans for converting the parish.

Young and Old

In his recent book on Youth Culture and the Gospel, Pete Ward describes an exciting ministry with unchurched young people from working-class estates in Oxford. They have had no previous contact with the Church. The question he poses is what will happen when these new young Christians do come to church. He invites us to imagine a group of goths or punks turning up in full rig-out at the local church. What is the way forward? Do they become a separate fringe or alternative church, or negotiate some compromise with one of the more open local churches? I recall that the lively and memorable welcome given to me in the Wakefield diocese by the young people was very far removed from what the average church member would find acceptable as an act of worship; but it was a clear indication of an important bridge that really must be crossed in this decade.

All the talk about youth culture must not lead the Church to forget the elderly. Perhaps it is because my middle name is Simeon that I warm greatly to the fact that the very first public witness to Jesus was given by the elderly Simeon. I was reminded recently that he and Anna were ready to receive Jesus because they had not sat back in their later years and retired spiritually. They had time for God in a way that the very busy do not. The huge increase in the number of older people provides the Church with an evangelistic opportunity that is largely overlooked. One of the chief privileges of ministry is to prepare the dying for their death. Although there are times when it will be appropriate for that ministry to be priestly, much of it can be done by the laity too. Growing old can be a lonely business, especially if you are on your own. It can be lonely even amongst other people in a residential or nursing home. As we near the end of our earthly life and prepare to meet our Lord we need, perhaps more than at any other time, to hear the good news of Jesus and to clasp his hand.

What Next?

'All of us will stand before God to be judged by him . . . Every one of us, then, will have to give an account of himself to God', says Paul in Romans 14:10, 12. In many churches it is unfashionable to preach about judgement, but I do believe that one day we will have to give an account of our life. One of the spiritual writers of this century who has influenced me is Geoffrey Studdert-Kennedy, the famous chaplain of the First World War. In the thick of the fighting and mud of the trenches, he proclaimed the Gospel by being alongside the dying – handing them a Woodbine and trying to help them on their last journey. In one of his dialect poems a soldier dreams he has died and

finds himself face to face with "Im'. His whole life flashes
before him and, for a moment, he recognises in God's eyes the
eyes of a London prostitute:

> And they was sad, – my Gawd 'ow sad,
> Wiv tears what seemed to shine,
> And quivering wi' the speech o' light
> They said, "Er soul was Mine.'
> And then at last 'E said one word,
> 'E just said one word – 'Well?'
> And I said in a funny voice,
> 'Please can I go to 'Ell?' . . .
> . . . There ain't no throne, and there ain't no books,
> It's 'Im you've got to see,
> It's 'Im, just 'Im, that is the Judge
> Of blokes like you and me.
> And, boys, I'd sooner frizzle up,
> I' the flames of a burnin' 'Ell,
> Than stand and look into 'Is face,
> And 'ear 'Is voice say – 'Well?'

Well?

How committed are the members of the Church of England to
proclaiming the Gospel in this Decade of Evangelism? The
early signs have been very encouraging. An amazing number
of congregations have been inspired to follow the bishops' call
'to make known by word and deed the love of the crucified
and risen Christ in the power of the Holy Spirit, so that people
will repent, believe and receive Christ as their Saviour and
obediently serve Him as their Lord in the fellowship of His
Church'.

Evangelism is firmly on the theological agenda in a way it
has rarely been before. In his substantial work, *Transforming
Mission*, David Bosch gives a definition of evangelism which
has been much praised and widely used:

Evangelism is that dimension and activity of the Church's mission which, by word and deed, and in the light of particular conditions and of a particular context, offers each person and community everywhere a valid opportunity to be directly challenged to a radical re-orientation of their lives, a re-orientation which involves such things as deliverance from slavery to the world and its powers; embracing Christ as Saviour and Lord; becoming a living member of his community, the church; being enlisted in his service of reconciliation, peace and justice on earth, and being committed to God's purpose of placing all things under the rule of Christ.

That all this must be firmly based on prayer is increasingly understood. Proclaiming the Gospel is about our own spiritual journey before it is about anything else. As Thomas Merton, the contemplative Trappist monk, who loved and understood all kinds of people and had a deep concern for justice, put it earlier this century:

Without contemplation and interior prayer the Church cannot fulfil her mission to transform and save mankind. Without contemplation she will be reduced to being the servant of cynical and worldly powers, no matter how hard her faithful may protest that they are fighting for the kingdom of God.

Jesus called his disciples to be the salt of the earth, but that does not mean we are expected to convert the whole world into a salt mine! We are to be the salt and to make sure we do not lose our saltiness (Matthew 5:13). It only takes a little salt to make all the difference.

A little incident which took place in Sophiatown when Trevor Huddleston was a parish priest there demonstrates this. Whenever he met a woman, no matter who she was, Trevor would always raise his hat to her. One day the young Desmond Tutu saw him do this to a black woman. That simple act so impressed Desmond Tutu that he became an active member of the Christian Church. As he was to say later, a faith which led a white man to raise his hat to a black woman must be worth following.

That was evangelism. That was proclaiming the Gospel of love and justice in a Christ-like way. Trevor Huddleston demonstrated what we all know to be true and would be wise to remember in this Decade of Evangelism: actions speak louder than words. As St Francis put it centuries earlier: 'Go into the world and proclaim the gospel. Use words if you have to.'

I know from my own ministry as a pastor and evangelist, that there are times when words must be used, and there is one verse to which I always return: John 3:16. It sums up exactly what the Gospel is about: 'God so loved the world that he gave his only Son, that whoever believes in him should not perish but have eternal life.'

RESPONSE

When I survey the wondrous cross
On which the Prince of glory died,
My richest gain I count but loss,
And pour contempt on all my pride.

Forbid it, Lord, that I should boast
Save in the death of Christ my God;
All the vain things that charm me most,
I sacrifice them to his Blood.

See from his head, his hands, his feet,
Sorrow and love flow mingled down;
Did e'er such love and sorrow meet,
Or thorns compose so rich a crown?

Were the whole realm of nature mine,
That were an offering far too small;
Love so amazing, so divine,
Demands my soul, my life, my all.

ISAAC WATTS (1674–1748)

A GOSPEL TO PROCLAIM

We have a gospel to proclaim,
good news for men in all the earth;
the gospel of a Saviour's name:
we sing his glory, tell his worth.

Tell of his birth at Bethlehem
not in a royal house or hall
but in a stable dark and dim,
the Word made flesh, a light for all.

Tell of his death at Calvary,
hated by those he came to save,
in lonely suffering on the cross,
for all he loved his life he gave.

Tell of that glorious Easter morn;
empty the tomb, for he was free:
he broke the power of death and hell
that we might share his victory.

Tell of his reign at God's right hand,
by all creation glorified.
He sends his Spirit on his church
to live for him, the Lamb who died.

Now we rejoice to name him King:
Jesus is Lord of all the earth.
This gospel-message we proclaim:
we sing his story, tell his worth.

EDWARD JOSEPH BURNS (1938–   )

Postscript

Once upon a time there was an Arab, who had three sons. One day he died and, in his will, he had left careful directions about how his property was to be divided between the sons. Everything was clear – until it came to the camels. There were seventeen. The instructions were that half of them were to go to the eldest son, a third to the middle son, and ninth to the youngest son. This presented the family with great problems. How could they possibly divide seventeen by two, three or nine?

They asked a neighbour for his advice. He was a wise old man and he said to them: 'I will lend you my camel, and then it will work out all right.' So the sons borrowed the neighbour's camel. That made eighteen camels. Now it was easy. The eldest son took half – that was nine. The second son took a third – that was six. The youngest son took a ninth – that was two. That, of course, came to seventeen, and they no longer needed the eighteenth camel.

The Decade of Evangelism is the eighteenth camel.